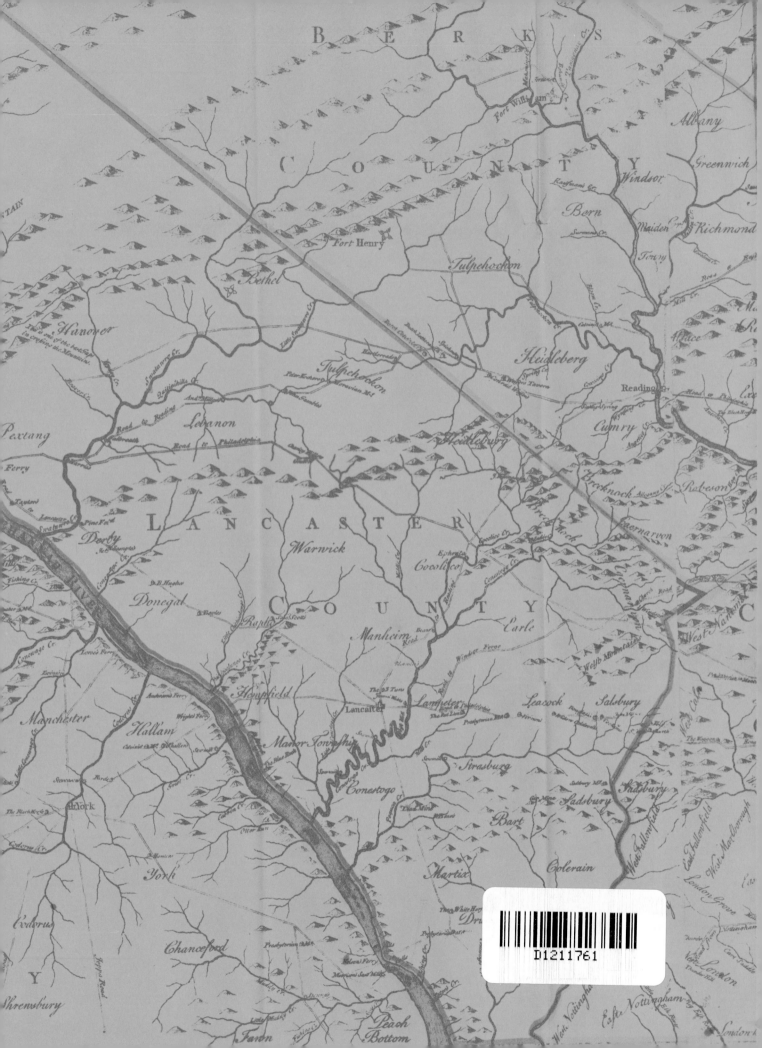

OLD LANCASTER

Charles X Carlson 1964

Frederic S. Klein
1964

OLD LANCASTER

Historic Pennsylvania Community

from its beginnings to 1865

Text by Frederic Shriver Klein

Art by Charles X. Carlson

with a foreword by

H. M. J. Klein

EARLY AMERICA SERIES, INC.

Lancaster, Pennsylvania

1 9 6 4

To

H. M. J. KLEIN

*in appreciation of his
pride in the past, his
achievements in the present,
and his optimism for the
future of his community.*

▼

Carlson

717-548 - 2231

After November

TABLE OF CONTENTS

PREFACE

Although most historical works originate with a narrative, to which appropriate illustrations are added, this book had its origin from an unusually fine collection of paintings and drawings. They were made by a talented artist who became interested in the unique story of the early community of Old Lancaster, and in the rich heritage of American history which remained in existence through the old homes, churches, schools, inns, bridges, shops and mills of the area, many of which have seen more than two hundred years of the American story.

For a number of years, Charles X. Carlson, with the advice and inspiration of Dr. H. M. J. Klein, a well-known historian and resident of Lancaster for more than half a century, visited, explored and sketched both familiar and little-known scenes of early events.

The result is apparent in the living history which these illustrations portray, because a fine artist's pen or brush can show impressions and ideas which the lens of a camera cannot duplicate. The decision to limit the scope of this book to the period before the 1860's was made because in later years the camera could and did picture scenes from the life of the people with indisputable accuracy. But, where buildings no longer exist, and where imagination is necessary to reconstruct events or conditions, this combination of narrative history and the artist's brush can describe aspects of early life which could easily be forgotten as they move further into the past with each passing year.

In the absence of any other general history of this period in print at the time of this writing, it seemed that these illustrations offered an unusual opportunity to provide a useful, accurate and coherent account of most of the major events and some of the minor aspects of the story of Old Lancaster, in combination with the imaginative historical scenes depicted by the artist.

All historical writing tends to reflect the particular interest and background of the historian, and the writing of regional history is subject to the same temptations as national history—the unconscious tendency to emphasize a locality or a state or a nation as being entirely unique. The author would be the last to claim that many of the experiences of this community were not shared by other communities in Pennsylvania, and in some of the oldest of the original colonies. But, as in every microcosm of history, some of the story of Old Lancaster is distinctive and unusual, and most of it is typical of an age that is rapidly receding into the past, and represents a heritage which should be preserved.

The combination of the most appropriate art with the most significant history has necessitated many decisions about the selection and organization of subject matter. Certain scenes and descriptions which would be necessary in a completely comprehensive reference work may not be found in this volume, but the combination which it does present should provide an attractive and useful cross-section of early life in Lancaster County.

Whether the reader will always agree with what is considered "artistic license" is never certain, but every effort has been made to insure reasonable accuracy along with permissible invention. Where buildings no longer exist, research into old narratives and the examination of early sketches has helped in the reconstruction. Where sources do not exist, everyone's imagination has equal merit. Histories are rarely complete and accurate in every detail, and if errors may have been made in the presentation of the narrative or the illustrations, it is hoped the reader will be charitable.

Special appreciation is expressed to William D. Andes, for the artistic design and layout of the pages of *Old Lancaster,* and all those associated with the production of this book acknowledge with gratitude the enthusiasm and encouragement given to this project by many interested individuals and organizations in the community.

Frederic Shriver Klein

Lancaster, Pennsylvania
February 12, 1964

OLD LANCASTER

FOREWORD

The United States is no longer a young nation. It has reached its maturity. In more recent years, scores of new nations have sprung up all over the globe.

This is one reason why the United States is becoming traditionally-minded. It is beginning to appreciate more than ever "the rock from which it was hewn and the well from which it was digged."

Faneuil Hall in Boston, the Federal Building in New York, and Independence Hall in Philadelphia mean more to us today than they ever did before. In the new frontiers in space we are not becoming unmindful of the old frontiers in time.

Lancaster County, Pennsylvania, has played an important role in the colonial and Federal days of our government. There is an Old Lancaster which goes back to several centuries of Indian lore, to the days of French traders and settlers, some of whom arrived here from the north in the days of Champlain. Early settlers came here in the days of William Penn when the area was still a part of the original Chester County. They came from Europe in the days when Queen Anne and William of the House of Orange still ruled in England and when Louis the Fourteenth of France devastated the Palatinate.

Robert Galt led the Scotch-Irish into the Pequea Valley. Hans Herr brought the Palatines, and Madame Ferree led the French Huguenots to the soil of what is now known as Lancaster County, Pennsyl-vania, in days when William Penn was still living, and bought their land from his descendants—land then known as Penn's Woods, and now known as the Garden Spot of America.

There is a Lancaster starting even before the county was separated from Penn's original Chester County and established as a distinct entity in 1729 and the townstead planned in 1730. This took place before George Washington was born or before the idea of a United States was even conceived.

The area was strategic, leading directly from the Atlantic to the Alleghenies and becoming a doorway to the west in the days of the French and Indian wars. By the time of the formation of our national life, Lancaster was the largest inland town in the United States—important enough to be considered worthy of becoming the capital of the United States, and as a matter of fact, having that honor for at least a day when the British occupied Philadelphia. Furthermore, it became the capital of the Commonwealth of Pennsylvania for more than a decade.

In the first half of the 19th century it played an important part in the cultural, social, economic and political life of the Commonwealth. After receiving a City Charter in 1818, Lancaster played an important part in our nation's expansion as hundreds of Conestoga wagons rumbled through the streets carrying cargo and immigrants to the new West.

In the wars of the Revolution, of 1812, of Mexico and of the Rebellion, Old Lancaster forms a gallant chapter.

Yes, there is an Old Lancaster of which we have a right to be proud. It has its own distinct architecture, culture and customs. It must be preserved for its own sake and for the sake of the New Lancaster which is rapidly developing. The old is the foundation of the new. It gives breadth, horizon, and stability to the new.

This, too, is conservation. How is the old to be preserved? One way is by restoring and preserving the actual buildings which have historic interest and value. Lancaster, fortunately, is doing this in the restoration of Wheatland, President Buchanan's home, Rock Ford, and the Fulton Theatre.

Another form of preservation, of equal and perhaps of more permanent value, is found in this beautifully illustrated history of Old Lancaster, the pages of which will remain after the structures themselves are gone. Too many of these historic structures have already disappeared, so the imagination must be used in restoring them.

This history of Old Lancaster is of rare value for many years to come. We have never had anything like it. The beautiful artistic work in this volume is the result of the brush of a skillful, talented, widely known artist who is a resident of Lancaster County and an enthusiastic devotee of its unique culture and history.

The far-sighted production of this work is to be commended. It is a wholesome sign, showing the interest of many persons in the preservation of cultural values.

J.H.M.J.Klein

PART ONE: INDIANS AND EARLY SETTLERS

to 1740

LONG BEFORE WHITE MEN came to Pennsylvania, the valley of the Susquehanna River was familiar territory to many of the Indian tribes of the east, who travelled along the river and its tributaries, hunting, fishing, fighting, and eventually setting up more or less permanent villages. The Pennsylvania area was usually in dispute between bands of Iroquois, who claimed most of the Susquehanna River as their own, and bands of Algonquins, who were more numerous to the north and northwest. In the area which was to become Lancaster County, the Susquehannocks, sometimes called Conestogas, were usually at war with the Iroquois, although they were closely related to them in racial origin. Other Indian tribes in the Lancaster area were Shawanese, Delawares, Conoys and Nanticokes, but most of these groups drifted away in later years.

When William Penn became proprietor of Pennsylvania, it seems probable that he visited the Indian tribes along the Susque-hanna River and became familiar with the area, because some years after he had planned his ideal city of Philadelphia, he made plans for another city along a Pennsylvania River in 1701, beginning at the mouth of the Conestoga Creek, and extending north along the Susquehanna for a distance of twelve miles. Unfortunately, Penn ran into financial troubles, and his plan did not materialize, or there might have been another city planned like old Philadelphia along the Susquehanna.

Early traders, both French and English, were the first white men to settle in the area, establishing friendly trade relations with the Indians, and bartering powder, blankets, and beads for valuable furs. Early colonial governors visited the Indian villages from time to time, to keep friendly relations and to make sure that the French were not exercising too much influence over the Indians.

When the first permanent white settlers arrived in the area in 1710, they found a well-established, peaceful Indian settlement in the southern portion of what was to become Lancaster County, with busy and prospering Indian traders, and fertile ground to be cultivated after the forests were cleared. After the first group of Mennonites came Huguenots from France, Scotch-Irish, Welsh, Quakers, Germans and English, and by 1729, when Lancaster County was formed, there were more than 3000 settlers in the area.

This part of Pennsylvania was originally part of Chester County, one of the three original counties, and settlers soon discovered that there were many inconveniences associated with the distance of almost one hundred miles which separated them from the nearest county seat at Chester. Courts, elections, constables were all far away; there was no attention to roads or bridges; outlaws and vagrants could evade the law by moving here, where there were no judges or jails. Following a petition by the inhabitants, Lancaster County was formed on May 10, 1729. The following year, on May 1, 1730, the townstead of Lancaster became the county seat of the new county.

Even in these early years, Indian trade and the expansion of settlements made the Lancaster community an important gateway for travel and transport to the west. Passing emigrants bought cattle, wagons, guns, trading articles, hardware and utensils to take on their journey to a pioneer home across the river.

Stage taverns and drover's taverns developed in the community. During the French and Indian Wars, Lancaster was chosen as the meeting place for Indian chiefs from all over the east and colonial governors from nearby colonies, to negotiate the great treaty which was to guarantee the loyalty of the Iroquois to the English.

By the middle of the 18th century the town and the county had begun to assume some of the characteristics which were to continue through its later history. There was a variety of national and religious groups who were able to preserve most of their culture and beliefs without interference from others; there were industrious farmers with fertile land to develop; there were skilled artisans and craftsmen who could manufacture the products which the new country needed; and commerce and transportation brought business opportunities for stores, merchants, innkeepers and tradesmen. This combination of agriculture, industry and commerce was to continue as the basis of the county's economy, and the independent spirit of its pioneer settlers, who had come to Pennsylvania to preserve their beliefs and traditions, was passed on to later generations, many of whom continued to live and work and worship in the homes and farmhouses and churches of their ancestors.

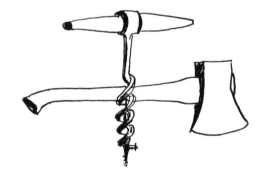

The Hans Herr House

The oldest house in Lancaster County is the Hans Herr House, still standing a few miles south of Lancaster, near Willow Street. Hans Herr led a Mennonite family into the Lancaster area in 1710, and one of his sons, Christian Herr, built a sturdy stone house in 1719 and carved the date over the doorway of the house. The Herr family were responsible for much of the Mennonite emigration from Europe into Pennsylvania, and many of their descendants still live in Lancaster County.

Hans Herr Brings a Colony of Mennonites

The families of Hans Herr, Martin Meylin, Martin Kendig and other Mennonites were part of thousands of Swiss Mennonite emigrants who had moved to England in the early 1700's, and then arrived in colonial New York, North Carolina and Pennsylvania. This group received a grant for about 10,000 acres of land near the Pequea Creek in 1710, and the land was subdivided among the families. Hans Herr, preacher for the first congregation, was chosen by lot to go back to Europe after the settlement had been established, to bring more emigrants to their new home in the New World, but his congregation felt that he was too important to spare, and another of the early settlers, Martin Kendig, made the trip and brought back new settlers for the community.

The First Europeans Come to the River Hills

Only a few years after the first English settlements were founded in North America, the great French explorer, Samuel de Champlain, sent his interpreter and guide, a young Frenchman named Etienne Brulé, to meet with Indian tribes in lands to the south of Canada. In 1618 Brulé reported to Champlain that he had explored the Susquehanna region to the sea. Sometime, more than three hundred years ago, Brulé's canoe, with his Indian guides, must have passed along the Susquehanna River, and the first European saw the river hills of Lancaster County.

The Beginnings of Indian Trade

Trade with the Indians was the beginning of commerce in the Lancaster County area. English, Swedish, Dutch and French traders set up trading posts along Pennsylvania rivers, to exchange beads, ribbons, knives, axes and liquor for furs. As early as 1630, a Virginian, William Claiborne, secured a license to trade with Indians and established a post near the mouth of the Susquehanna River. French traders had been on the Schuylkill and Brandywine rivers before coming to the Susquehanna. As competition between French and English developed, the French drew the fur trade toward the north, and the English encouraged the movement of furs down the Susquehanna toward southern Pennsylvania.

Traders dealt directly with the Indians, often marrying Indian wives, and acting as official agents for the tribe. The famous French trader, Martin Chartier, who had been with LaSalle in Illinois, established an important trading post near Washington Boro at the Pequea Creek, where he dealt with the Shawanee and Susquehannock Indians. Pennsylvania officials encouraged his activity, and he was given 300 acres of land near Pequea Creek, where he lived with his Indian wife until his death in 1718. The Pequea trading post was well known among the Indians, and both Chartier and his son Peter served as interpreters for the negotiations between Pennsylvania governors and the Indians.

The Pequea Trading Post

The Pequea trading post, south of Lancaster, was only one of several hundred which traders established in early 18th century Pennsylvania. Many of the traders were responsible for the establishment of early Pennsylvania towns which developed at the location of their trading stations, and early roads followed the path of the trails to and from the Indian trader's posts.

The Colonial Governor Comes to Confer with the Indians

Colonial governors frequently found it necessary to come to the great Indian town of the Susquehannocks, south of Lancaster, to confer about land boundaries, trading regulations, law violations, and particularly about the loyalty of the Indians to the English, rather than to the French.

In June, 1707, Governor John Evans, with his official party, came to spend several days with the Indian tribes near Pequea, where Chief Opessah greeted them with a salute of firearms. Regardless of promises to keep the peace, Indian raids and tribal wars caused much difficulty to the colonial government, and settlers were constantly complaining about Indian troubles. The importance of the fur trade made it necessary for the governor to be diplomatic with the Indians at the same time that he was placating the settlers.

The earliest permanent settlers of Lancaster County were a colony of Swiss Mennonites, who had emigrated from the mountains of Switzerland to the fields of the German Palatinate, and from there to Holland, England, and America. Followers of Menno Simons, they believed in complete separation of their church from the State, and had been persecuted and banished from many countries till they arrived in Pennsylvania in 1710. The fertile fields near the Pequea Creek resembled the farmlands of Palatinate Germany, and many of these Swiss-German families moved to Lancaster County in the early 18th century, to become the ancestors of many sixth or seventh generation descendants today who still live on some of the original tracts of land.

Other Swiss settlers were followers of Jacob Ammon, and became known as Amish. Their domestic discipline was more rigid, including strict emphasis on certain styles of clothing, and the wearing of beards. In general, all of the Anabaptist sects were known as the "Plain people," but there were many differences between very orthodox and very liberal groups, with the Old Order Amish remaining the most conservative.

The First Settlers: Swiss and German Palatines

The French Huguenots

French Huguenots, persecuted during the religious wars in France, found a haven in Pennsylvania at about the same time that the Swiss Mennonite settlers were emigrating. The pioneer of the Huguenot movement was the widow Mary Ferree, who took her family to England, secured the sympathy of William Penn and Queen Anne, and was able to bring her children to America in 1709. A few years later, the Ferree family found their way to the Pequea Valley area of Lancaster County, where they were greeted by the Indians, and established their home in the area near the present location of Paradise, where the Ferree graveyard remains today.

This one French Huguenot family, making a home in an Indian wilderness far from France, were the ancestors of a long succession of prominent Americans, active in law, government, academic and military life. General John Reynolds and Admiral Winfield Scott Schley are outstanding examples.

The Scotch-Irish

Many Scotch-Irish, from northern Ireland, were among the first settlers of the Lancaster County area. Hardy and aggressive, they were encouraged to settle along the frontier, and they established two colonies—one in the northwest area along the Chicques and the Octoraro, and one near the disputed Maryland border in the Drumore area, named for "Druim Muir" in Ireland. Several thousand of these sturdy pioneers were already in the area by the time Lancaster County was founded and they formed a strong bulwark against hostile Indians, Maryland squatters, and French enemies in the wars. They were devout in their religion, active in politics, and always full of determination to defend their individual rights.

The Peaceful Quakers

The Quakers found a welcome haven in Pennsylvania, in contrast to their unpopularity in most of the other colonies. Since Proprietor William Penn was a Quaker himself, members of the "Society of Friends" from England and from Holland and Germany were completely free in Pennsylvania to keep their religious views free from state control. Early settlements of Quakers were established at the old Sadsbury meetinghouse, at Penn Hill in the Little Britain area of southern Lancaster County, and in Drumore township. A group of Welsh Quakers made plans to establish a tremendous Quaker colony in Pennsylvania as soon as Penn secured his grant, and were allotted 40,000 acres of land, but disputed land titles broke up the project, and it never materialized.

Shortly after Lancaster County was established, Samuel Bethel's tavern, the *Sign of the Cross Keys,* on West King Street, became a favorite headquarters for Samuel Blunston, one of the early Quaker preachers, and the inn was later operated by Quakers. However, many of the Quakers were unpopular in frontier country because they opposed the payment of taxes for military purposes. They were among the very first settlers, and the *Cross Keys* was the second tavern to be licensed in the townstead.

The Quakers took an active part in government, and many political matters were discussed at this convenient location near the Court House. John Wright, one of the founders of the County, was a prominent Quaker leader in local and provincial government.

Building
the
Early Settlements

Forests rich with virgin chestnut, oak, walnut and pine made the building of settler's cabins and roadside inns a simple task for men who were familiar with the broad-axe and adze. Resting on a firm foundation of stones, hardwood logs, carefully notched at the ends with a few blows of an axe, flattened on two sides with an adze or broad-axe, were speedily erected into a structure which might not contain a single ounce of metal, but which would stand for a century without any signs of weakness. Chinks between the logs were plastered shut with clay, and shingles or "shakes" were split from blocks of chestnut with a mallet and shingle-knife, or "frou," to provide a sturdy roof for fifty years. The chimney could be built of stone or logs covered with clay, a solid floor made of half-logs, a water-supply provided by digging a well about five feet wide and fifteen or twenty feet deep, lining it with stone and hanging a bucket and rope at the top.

If a blacksmith, or water-powered pit-saw were nearby, further refinements could be added. Hand-made nails could fasten oak clapboards to the outside walls, hinges could hang pine doors, and a variety of household conveniences, from pothooks to pokers, could be added. Many of these original log structures, covered over for many generations with various types of exterior sheathing, still remain beneath a modern covering in many parts of the county.

Fences for livestock were easy to construct with locust posts and rails, or by the ingenious zig-zag "worm" fences that could be erected without digging post-holes. Out-buildings for horses and cattle, or log barns for storage of hay and grain soon followed construction of the dwelling, and the settler's forest home was complete.

Lancaster County is Formed

When Lancaster County was formed from part of Chester County in 1729, as the fourth county of Pennsylvania, one of the commissioners who had been appointed to survey the boundaries of the new county was John Wright, one of the earliest settlers, and the founder of Wright's Ferry, crossing the Susquehanna River. Wright had come from Lancashire, England, and was responsible for the suggestion that the name Lancaster should be given to the new county, in honor of his native soil.

When the new county was formed, it included all the land in Pennsylvania west of the three original counties, but in later years, as western migration continued, parts of it were made into York, Cumberland, Berks, Northumberland, Dauphin and Lebanon counties. Like their namesake shires in England, the red rose of the English House of Lancaster, and the white rose of the English House of York became symbols associated with the two counties which bordered on the Susquehanna River.

Since 1813 there were no more changes in the boundaries of the county, which then enclosed nine hundred and forty-five square miles, extending about forty-one miles north and south, and about forty-five miles east and west.

The First Court
at
Postlethwaite's Tavern

When Lancaster County was founded in 1729, the main road from Philadelphia to the Susquehanna River was the Old Conestoga Road, passing through Gap and about four miles south of Lancaster, past Postlethwaite's Tavern, an important public-house in the Indian trading region. John Postlethwaite invited the first courts to meet here, beginning August 5, 1729. The first case was the trial of a thief, who was sentenced to "be publicly whipped on the bare back with twenty-one stripes, well laid on."

Hickory Town Becomes the Borough of Lancaster

The location of a county seat for the new county would have seemed logical at either Postlethwaite's Tavern or at Wright's Ferry, now Columbia. The final site which became Lancaster lay about half-way between the old Conestoga Road to the south, and the old "Peter's Road," passing north near Manheim. However, Andrew Hamilton, a Philadelphia lawyer, with his son James Hamilton, secured a tract of land in the vicinity of George Gibson's *Hickory Tree* tavern, and planned to lay out a town, with lots provided for a Court House, a market and a jail. The trustees approved Hamilton's location, and "Hickory Town" soon became Lancaster, the county seat of Lancaster County. It is believed that Gibson's tavern was located a short distance east of the present square.

PART TWO: PERSONALITIES AND PATRIOTS
1740–1800

During the French and Indian wars, in the middle of the eighteenth century, Lancaster was the most important gateway to the west, with new settlers and soldiers passing through it in growing numbers, buying their supplies, wagons, rifles, and cattle, and then moving on to cross the Susquehanna River into territory that often became the scene of Indian warfare. News of border conflicts usually arrived in Lancaster first, and was carried from here to the colonial government at Philadelphia, and the great Indian Treaty of 1744 at Lancaster indicated that it was the best meeting place for Indians and government officials at that time.

Although Indian warfare did not reach Lancaster County, the resentment of white settlers in Paxtang, near Harrisburg, resulted in a cruel massacre of a peaceful tribe of Conestoga Indians in Lancaster in 1763, when raiders came into town and exterminated the men, women and children of the last remaining Lancaster County Indians.

At the outbreak of the Revolution, Lancaster riflemen were among the first to march to Boston, armed with the famous long rifles for which the county was already well known, and large groups of local volunteers, led by Colonel Edward Hand, participated with Washington's army in the New York and New Jersey campaigns. Large quantities of supplies for the patriot army were provided from Lancaster County, where a number of iron furnaces and forges produced cannon and ammunition, farms supplied grain, and local tradesmen and craftsmen furnished uniforms, shoes, rifles, and even the camp kettles for the army at Valley Forge.

During the war, British and Hessian prisoners were sent to various parts of the county, where they were far enough away from the scenes of battle to be secure from rescue or escape. Many of the Hessian prisoners remained in the local German community, to marry and become part of the new nation. Most famous of the British prisoners was young Major André, who lived in Lancaster for some time as a paroled prisoner before his execution as a spy for Benedict Arnold.

Many prominent personalities were associated with Lancaster while the new nation was being formed. George Ross, a signer of the Declaration of Independence, was a resident of Lancaster. Washington, Lafayette and Thomas Paine were entertained in the town on various occasions. David Ramsay, the first historian of the Revolution, and William Henry, gunsmith and member of the Continental Congress were well-known figures in the new national government. Perhaps the most distinguished citizen was General Edward Hand, who had become Adjutant-General under Washington. When he was elected Chief Burgess of the city in 1789, General Hand proposed to Congress that Lancaster would be a fitting location for the new capital of the nation and stated that among its many qualifications were a population of about 4,200 persons in the largest inland town in the United States, five public buildings, many large and elegant houses, and industries which included 14 hatters, 36 shoemakers, 25 tailors, 7 gunsmiths, 3 printing presses and 40 houses of public entertainment for travellers.

The forty public-houses, or taverns must have provided a distinctive and colorful atmosphere to Old Lancaster by the turn of the century, with their gaily painted tavern signs or emblems hanging in successive locations as one gazed down the main streets. Some contained portraits, like Washington or Pitt; some depicted symbols, like the Fountain or the Conestoga Wagon, and many displayed an object, like the massive iron bunch of grapes, for the *Grape Tavern,* or a hat or pair of crossed keys. Stagecoaches brought news, mail and papers to the inns; travellers arrived and departed; public meetings, theatrical performances and social affairs were held there. In many other early American towns, built along rivers or the seacoast, most of the contact with the rest of the world came by boat or ship in the dock area, but in Lancaster, as an inland town, a constant stream of overland traffic, by great freight wagons, stage-coaches and private carriages brought increased importance to the tavern.

Lancaster had been the capital of the nation for one day, in 1777, when Congress met there after fleeing from Philadelphia. It became the capital of Pennsylvania on two occasions, and the new Court House in the square became the State House. Churches of all denominations existed in the town and the county, and Franklin College had been established in 1787, with the financial help and encouragement of Benjamin Franklin, becoming the third college in the state of Pennsylvania.

Thomas Cookson Becomes the First Burgess

Thomas Cookson, Chief Burgess

Thomas Cookson, one of the early settlers, was appointed Chief Burgess when the village became the Borough of Lancaster in 1742. Among the first acts of the burgesses were restrictions preventing shopkeepers and tavernkeepers from conducting business on Sunday, regulations against riding horse races through the town, against playing ball at the Court House, and against riding horses on the sidewalks. There was also a law prohibiting citizens from allowing pigs to run loose on East King Street, or firing guns in the streets. Market days were established twice a week on Wednesdays and Saturdays, and the boundaries of the town were described as extending one mile in each direction from Penn Square. The boundaries remained unchanged until the mid-twentieth century.

The Monastic Community at Ephrata

A Kitchen

A Stone Wash Trough

One of the most unique institutions in America was established in the 1730's at Ephrata, when a young German named Conrad Beissel founded an Old World monastic community, known as the Ephrata Cloister. As the little congregation grew, men and women, known as "Brothers" and "Sisters" lived in isolation from the world, enduring strict discipline and physical hardships, but the Ephrata community produced some of the first choral music in America, and its printing press and illuminated manuscripts were an important contribution to colonial culture.

The architecture of the cloister buildings was distinctively foreign, with extremely steep roofs, notched logs covered with grey clapboards, and floor beams extending through the wall to the outside. The Saal, or prayer house, and the adjoining Sister's House were the first buildings, but the community grew to several hundred, and a little group of other buildings was added to the settlement, including a special house for Beissel, the founder.

Life in the cloister was severe, with the members of the "Camp of the Solitary" living in tiny cells, equipped only with a wooden bench and a block of wood for a pillow. Doorways were made only five feet high and twenty inches wide, to teach humility and the narrowness of the road to salvation. There were midnight prayer services, and the day began at four o'clock in the morning and lasted till nine o'clock at night, divided between prayer and work.

The Ephrata printing press at the Cloister was one of the first presses in the province, and its imprints have become rare and valuable publications. One of its most famous productions was the "Martyr's Book," which is considered one of the finest examples of early American printing. During the Revolutionary War, soldiers were sent to the Cloister paper mill for cartridge paper, but not finding a sufficient quantity, they took printed sheets from the press, and used the religious tracts to fire bullets at the battle of Germantown.

Some of the first choral music in America was produced at Ephrata Cloisters, when Superintendent Beissel and others began composing, writing and singing hymns and anthems, based on a distinctive seven-note harmony. Beissel's singing school rehearsed rigidly for four hours nightly, and he insisted on the wearing of robes by the choir, and even recommended a special diet for his singers, declaring that the eating of fruit and meat, and the drinking of milk, were injurious to the human voice. The choirs rewarded his efforts by presenting him with two beautifully ornamented music books, each containing more than five hundred hand-written compositions.

The Cloister

The Bake House at Ephrata Cloister

Colonial Officials Come to Treat with the Indians

In 1744, several hundred Indians and Indian chiefs met in Lancaster with representatives of the Governors of Pennsylvania, Maryland and Virginia for an important conference which settled many disputes between the Six Nations and the English, and guaranteed that the Indians would not join with the French in the border war. The meetings were held in the old Court House in the square, and a complete Indian village was set up on the edge of town.

For two weeks, from June 22 to July 4, colonial leaders bargained with gaily painted Indian chieftains, offering trade goods like gunpowder, shot, jewsharps, blankets, guns and shirts, along with the customary supply of rum, in exchange for Indian land claims in Virginia and Maryland, and the promise that they would ally themselves with the English. With the assistance of Conrad Weiser as interpreter, Indian leaders inspected goods, examined crude maps, made lengthy speeches, exchanged belts of wampum after each speech, and applauded, according to their custom, by shouting "Jo-Hah!"

During the period of the conference, families from the Indian village explored the streets of Old Lancaster, traded with the settlers at the old market house, and held lengthy pow-wows around their cooking-fires during the summer evenings, discussing the progress of the day's conference.

Finally, after much drinking of healths and a final bonus of rum, Chief Canassetaga was presented with a scarlet coat from the Virginians, and Chief Gachadow received a bold-laced hat from the Maryland commissioners, and the Indians packed up their wigwams and families and departed with their dogs and horses. The "Great Treaty of 1744" ended Indian claims to thousands of acres of land, and protected Pennsylvania from serious Indian raids during the French War of 1744–1748.

The Great Indian Treaty of 1744

Indian chiefs from many tribes of the Six Nations bargained excitedly with colonial leaders in Lancaster in 1744, finally surrendering large land claims to the whites, and becoming allies.

Indians Trade at the Old Market

During two weeks of Indian negotiations, a large Indian camp was set up on the edge of the town, and Indians mingled with townsfolk in shops and at the old market house, hoping to find a good bargain.

Paxtang Settlers Massacre the Conestoga Indians

Angered by accounts of border Indian raids during the years of the French and Indian War, a group of settlers from Paxtang, in the Harrisburg area, decided to wipe out the small encampment of Conestoga Indians remaining south of Lancaster. After their first attack on the 14th of December, 1763, remaining Indian families were moved to the old jail on Water Street in Lancaster for protection, but on December 27th, the "Paxtang Boys" rode into town, broke open the doors to the jail and massacred men, women and children, before the Sheriff and local citizens could stop them. The peaceful camp of Lancaster Indians at Indiantown was no more, for this was the last remaining tribe of Indians in the county.

Count Zinzendorf Founds a Moravian Community

*First Gemeinhaus in Lititz:
1744*

Count Zinzendorf

Count Zinzendorf, the founder of the Moravian movement, and its most famous missionary, came to Lititz and Lancaster in 1742, preaching the importance of evangelical work among the settlers and the Indians. Moravian friendship with the Indians was not approved by other settlers, and on one occasion a Lancaster congregation was startled by the sight of "savages, appearing at the church windows with their swarthy faces and with knives in their hands."

Indian Trade Becomes Big Business for Joseph Simon

One of the largest landholders in colonial Pennsylvania, and the most prominent Indian trader was Joseph Simon, who came to Lancaster in 1740 and operated a trading store in the square. Simon travelled widely through the Ohio and Illinois country, supplying trade goods to many stores and western traders. He became one of the wealthiest men in Pennsylvania, and participated actively in the civic affairs of early Lancaster.

There had been a small colony of Jewish settlers at nearby Schaefferstown for some years, and a number of Jewish traders involved in the Indian trade, but Simon was one of the most successful, and the most respected. He survived an Indian attack at Bloody Run, along with Alexander Lowry and other partners in 1763, and in his later years, when the partners were arranging an accounting of their long years of Indian trade, it is said that, without books or records, the two partners reminded each other of sums of money paid to each other many years past, sitting together on a log in the forest, or resting at a spring somewhere in the western woods.

Joseph Simon's grand-daughter, Rebecca Gratz, became a resident of Philadelphia, and the friendship of some of her associates with Sir Walter Scott is believed to have been responsible for Scott's descriptions of the character and appearance of "Rebecca" in the novel, "Ivanhoe."

Martin Meylin Makes Pennsylvania Rifles

Early settlers from Europe may have been familiar with European sporting rifles and smoothbore military muskets, but few Europeans owned their own guns. However, life in the new world, particularly in isolated areas, made a personal fire-arm a necessity, where free hunting and unlimited game for food existed, and where protection from Indians, outlaws and savage animals had to be provided for the family. Settlers who passed through Lancaster on their way to the west needed firearms, and craftsmen in the area developed a special type of American rifle for their needs. Gunsmiths like Meylin, Stengel, Young, Ferree, and Henry made and rifled their own gun-barrels, selected fine grained wood for gunstocks, and decorated their handwork with elaborate brass fittings, plates and patchboxes. The range and accuracy of the famous Pennsylvania rifle were due to the precision of the rifling, the fit of the rifleball, and the proper type of greased buckskin or linen patch to seal the rifling grooves against escaping powder gases.

The new type of weapon, designed for personal use, became a deadly military rifle in the Revolution, when used by Pennsylvania riflemen against the short-range, inaccurate smoothbore muskets of the British army, and Lancaster became known as an "armorer's town" because of the many rifles made here for Washington's army.

Martin Meylin, one of the early Mennonite settlers in the region just south of Lancaster, may very well have been the first colonist to transform the heavy, large-calibre European rifles into the distinctive, graceful and accurate Pennsylvania, or Lancaster, rifle, which became the characteristic American firearm throughout the next century.

Elizabeth Furnace

A German Emigrant Becomes a Pennsylvania "Baron"

One of the most colorful characters of colonial Pennsylvania was William Henry Stiegel, ironmaster and manufacturer of fine glassware at Elizabeth Furnace. He founded the town of Manheim, and lived in the style of a European nobleman, which gave him the unofficial title of "Baron" Stiegel.

Shortly after his arrival from Europe, young Heinrich Stiegel married Elizabeth Huber, the daughter of ironmaster Huber, who operated Elizabeth Furnace, near what was to become the town of Manheim. After some years of experience, he bought the furnace from his father-in-law, and expanded his operations rapidly, acquiring thousands of acres of land and several other furnaces.

The Stiegel Office in Manheim

About 1761, after having been in America for ten years, Stiegel and his partners laid out the town of Manheim, and built a large brick mansion in 1765. This imposing structure, in a tiny settlement, led to the unofficial title of "Baron," for his wealth

Stiegel Laying out Manheim

and activities led to a life of baronial splendor. The house contained a special chapel, in which Stiegel occasionally preached to his workmen, and on the high roof, between the chimneys, was a large balcony on which, on some occasions, an orchestra of European musicians entertained his guests, or greeted the arrival of the "Baron" as he approached the town in a magnificent coach. Sometimes the firing of a cannon on a high tower announced his arrival to the workmen.

The mansion house at Elizabeth Furnace, a few miles north-east of the town, was an imposing stone structure, and part of the building was used as a barracks for prisoners during the Revolutionary war, when they could be employed as workmen for the iron manufacturers. Stiegel imported European workmen to produce the famous Stiegel glass at a large factory in Manheim, and the formula which resulted in the beautiful colors and shades of his glassware has never been matched.

Stiegel was a devout Lutheran, and when a new church had to be built in Manheim, he deeded the land to the church for an annual quitrent of "One Red Rose," a fee which is still presented annually as a community tradition.

Over-speculation led to financial disaster for Stiegel, and in 1774 his property was seized and he spent a short time in a debtor's prison. Robert Morris, financier of the American Revolution, bought Stiegel's Manheim mansion, and Stiegel was employed as a foreman at his own Elizabeth Furnace during the Revolution. Shortly afterwards he left the vicinity, taught school for a brief period, and died at the age of fifty-six, unaware that his name would be associated for centuries with some of the finest examples of early American craftsmanship in glassware.

Benjamin Franklin Comes to Buy Wagons

In 1755, when the French and Indian War brought the danger of savage border war to Pennsylvania, Benjamin Franklin was authorized to find wagons and horses for the supplies of Braddock's army, on its march against Fort Duquesne. Franklin came to Lancaster, well-known even at that time for its famous wagon-makers, and secured a large number, laden with grain and forage, for the army. The army reported that they were by far the best of any that had been supplied since their arrival in America.

The Boston Port Bill Brings a Merchants' Boycott

The decision of the British Parliament in 1774 to punish Massachusetts for the "Boston Tea Party" brought about the "Boston Port Bill" and quickly aroused protests from all the colonies.

Probably the first meeting of Revolutionary patriots in Lancaster took place at the Court House on the 15th of June, when they resolved that they would boycott trade with Great Britain, and urge all the merchants, traders and manufacturers in the town to join in association with them. A Committee of Correspondence was formed to correspond with Philadelphia patriots, and shortly afterwards, formal resolves were printed and a large public meeting held at the Court House on July 9th, 1774. With George Ross as chairman, they proclaimed their allegiance to the British Crown, but denounced the British Parliament as having been "unconstitutional, unjust and oppressive."

Meetings and resolutions like this all over the colonies brought many communities together in a common cause, and the organization of patriotic groups to suppress violators of the boycott agreements followed quickly. In Lancaster, in August of that year, two merchants were charged by the committee with having imported a chest of British tea, but after investigation it was determined that the tea had been smuggled into the country without payment of the tax, and the merchants were dismissed.

**Patriots Are
Called to Arms
at the
Grape Hotel**

Established in 1742, the *Grape* Hotel, in the first block of North Queen St., with its large bunch of grapes as its tavern sign, was the scene of many meetings of Revolutionary patriots during the 1770's. Citizens met here immediately after news of the Battle of Lexington, to organize companies of volunteer militia. The *Grape* was a favorite dining place for James Buchanan in later years.

A few days after the news of Lexington reached Lancaster, a meeting of citizens was held on April 27th, 1775 at the *Grape* Hotel, whose proprietor was Adam Reigart. Within a few days, the *Grape* Hotel had become the headquarters of the Lancaster Committee of Observation, and plans were made to raise companies of one hundred volunteers each, and to make a survey of the available powder and lead in the community.

The First Fourth of July

The adoption of the Declaration of Independence was not a great surprise to Lancaster. George Ross, of Lancaster, was a member of the Congress, and Lancaster riflemen had been fighting in New England and on Long Island for many months. The British invasion of New York in June brought about the need for reinforcements for Washington's armies. On July 1st, the first volunteer companies of riflemen were re-enlisted as the First Regiment, Pennsylvania Line, under General Edward Hand. Congress ordered a "Flying Camp" of ten thousand men to be organized at once in the middle colonies, and Lancaster was selected to be the meeting place for the representatives of all the militia companies in the state, on a day that was to become historic—the Fourth of July, 1776. George Ross was president of the meeting.

Officers and privates from fifty-three battalions, representing many areas of Pennsylvania, gathered to elect Daniel Roberdeau first Brigadier-General, and pledge to march under the direction of their officers to the assistance of "any of the free, independent states of America."

However, news of the actual adoption of the Declaration of Independence did not reach Lancaster for several days, and it was not until July 8th that the proclamation was formally read.

An Oath of Allegiance at the Donegal Witness Tree

When Scotch-Irish Presbyterians came to Pennsylvania shortly after 1700, a small congregation built a log meeting house at Donegal Spring, near the Chicques Creek. About 1740, the present Donegal church was built of rough stone which had been gathered in the vicinity, the inside walls were plastered, and the little congregation worshipped in the unheated, unpainted interior for many years until it was re-modelled in 1851.

A dramatic scene took place during the Revolutionary War beneath the giant oak tree which still stands at the church. On a Sunday morning in 1777, a courier rode up to notify Colonel Alexander Lowry that the Donegal Battalion was needed to help repel the British invasion near Philadelphia. The men gathered under the oak tree, with their reluctant Tory pastor, Rev. Mc-Farquhar, to pledge their allegiance to the Revolutionary cause.

Gunpowder is Stored in the Government Powder-House

During the final years of the French and Indian Wars, when Indian raids threatened much of the Susquehanna Valley, the provincial government selected Lancaster for the location of military barracks and associated buildings for the use of troops which might have to be sent to trouble spots along the frontier. A military barracks and stables were built at North Duke and Walnut Streets by 1768, but the frontier wars had ended by this time. With the outbreak of the Revolution, the State used these properties, and a government warehouse on Queen Street near James, along with a stone powder-house on Duke Street near James, for war purposes. Lancaster was far enough away from the scene of early conflict to be a safe location for storage of guns, uniforms and equipment, and for large quantities of gunpowder. During the war, British and Hessian prisoners were quartered in the barracks, and local militia were usually assigned to guarding both the powder-house and the prisoners stationed in the town.

The powder-house was constructed by authorization from John Hubley, a Lancaster lawyer who was a delegate to the Congress in 1776, and was appointed as Commissary for the army in 1777. Among Hubley's assignments was the employment of all the shoemakers among the Hessian prisoners to make shoes for the troops. The magazine for storage of powder was to be twenty-four by thirty-six feet in size. On one occasion Hubley was ordered to supply enough gunpowder to make up 20,000 musket charges. Hubley's account books in the first years of the war show frequent items for expenses in "entertaining riflemen," when rifle companies were being formed to go to Boston.

**Archibald Steele
Leads the March
against Quebec**

One of the Scotch-Irish patriots in southern Lancaster County was Col. Archibald Steele, who walked from Lancaster to Boston after the war broke out at Lexington and Concord. With six companions, he led the advance scouts of Montgomery's expedition against Quebec, and fought with Continental troops in that engagement. Steele became head of the Commissary, and of the Philadelphia Arsenal.

Col. Steele joined General Arnold's little army in September, 1775, along with seventeen-year old John Joseph Henry, the runaway son of William Henry, Lancaster gunsmith. Going up to the mouth of the Kennebec River in Maine, Steele and six men, including young Henry, were sent ahead as scouts to locate the Indian trails and find the way to Quebec. Unable to use their guns to shoot game, for fear of being detected, the little party suffered severe hardships from hunger and cold, but their mission was accomplished.

Thomas Paine is not a Welcome Guest

Thomas Paine, author of the violent political writings which aroused the colonists to the movement for independence in 1776, was a resident of Lancaster in 1777 and 1778, as the guest of William Henry, gunsmith and prominent patriot, but Paine's personal behavior was not admired as much as his famous writings under the name of "Common Sense."

Henry's son, Judge John Joseph Henry, described Paine as an "atheist and a maniac, who should have been in a madhouse." According to his description, Paine loafed about in the mornings, spent two or three hours at dinner, then wrapped himself in a blanket for a nap in an armchair for the rest of the afternoon. Occasionally he wrote two or three lines for his pamphlet, "The Crisis," but he acquired the general reputation of being an egotistical, lazy, immoral and slovenly guest. The disapproval of his fellow-citizens was shown by an incident in Philadelphia, when a group of Lancaster patriots had attended an official banquet. On Market Street they saw Paine coming toward them. "There comes 'Common Sense,'" said one of them. "D-n him!" said Matthias Slough, "I'll 'Common Sense' him!" whereupon he tripped him and threw him into the gutter!

Paine became a bitter critic of Washington in later years because he disapproved of Washington's association with the aristocratic Federalist party.

Paine had returned to Europe during the days of the French Revolution, and became as enthusiastic about the uprising of the French people as he had been about American independence, which he felt had been betrayed by the propertied classes in America when the powerful Federalist party gained control of the government after the Constitution had been adopted.

Major André is a Paroled Prisoner in Lancaster

When captured British prisoners were sent to Lancaster from the Canadian campaign of 1775, a young man named John André arrived with them, and lived at the Caleb Cope House on North Lime Street, near Grant Street, for almost four months. Like many prisoners, he gave his word of honor not to go near any seaport town nor farther than six miles from Lancaster, and consequently was paroled and free to live in the town without restrictions. André was a pleasant and talented young man of twenty-four at the time, and enjoyed himself with the five young sons of Caleb Cope, who had been Burgess of Lancaster, teaching them painting and drawing, and taking part in their games and sports.

André was exchanged with other prisoners, and rejoined the British Army, rising to the post of Adjutant-general of the British Forces in America, but his unfortunate involvement with Benedict Arnold eventually led to his capture with incriminating papers, and his execution as a spy in 1780. His remains were buried in Westminster Abbey.

Baron von Steuben Goes to a Ball

Baron von Steuben, the German nobleman who volunteered to serve in the Continental Army, and who introduced an original military system of regulations and soldierly discipline into the troops of Washington's informal army, was formally entertained in Lancaster on February 19, 1778, on his return from a meeting with the Continental Congress at York.

A citizen's committee met Steuben and formally welcomed him to the nation's "largest inland city," and arranged a ball for the distinguished visitor that evening. It was reported that Steuben was surprised and delighted to find that so many of the young ladies of Lancaster were able to converse fluently in the German language.

Steuben was largely responsible for the beginnings of efficiency in the American military system. He insisted that officers take personal responsibility for the actions of their troops, instead of leaving all supervision to sergeants. His detailed regulations

for the manual of arms and procedures for loading and firing muskets simplified and shortened the thirteen commands and motions formerly required to load and fire the soldiers' weapons.

Lititz Becomes a Hospital Town for the Wounded

The Moravians and their leader Count Zinzendorf were responsible for the founding of the Lititz community, named after a town in Bohemia. At the time of the Revolution, the Moravian church owned the entire town, and its many buildings, including the Brother's House and the Sister's House made up most of the main portion of the settlement.

In December, 1777, orders came from General Washington that two hundred and fifty sick and wounded Revolutionary soldiers would have to be quartered in Lititz. After an inspection, the Brethren's House was approved as a hospital, and during the next few days, wagons full of wounded soldiers from the New Jersey campaigns began rolling into town. After the first few days, the temporary hospital was filled, and some of the patients had to be cared for elsewhere in the community. The wounded were cared for in Lititz for many months, until August, 1778, when the remaining patients were transferred and the hospital was closed. Hospitals for wounded soldiers were also established at Ephrata, Manheim and Reamstown during the Revolution.

General Hand Lives at Rock Ford after the War

A fine old Georgian mansion a few miles south of Lancaster was the residence of General Edward Hand, Adjutant-General of the Revolutionary Army and one of Washington's closest friends.

Hand came to America as a young surgeon with an Irish regiment that came to Philadelphia at the close of the French and Indian wars. He spent some time at Fort Pitt, where frontier attacks were imminent, but in 1774, at the outbreak of the Revolution, he resigned from the British Army, and came to Lancaster to practice medicine. He married a Lancaster girl the following year, and when fighting broke out in Massachusetts, Hand joined the army again, this time with the colonists to fight against the British. He was one of the first Americans to understand the importance of the Pennsylvania rifle as a military weapon, and his 1st Regiment of Pennsylvania

Riflemen were the most valuable and dangerous of the troops under Washington's command.

A long and prominent military career lasted until 1783 and took Hand and his family to other parts of the country before his return to Lancaster at the end of the war. As Chief Burgess of Lancaster in 1789, he urged Congress to select the city as the new capital of the United States, and entertained George Washington when he visited Lancaster in 1791.

General Hand purchased the land on which Rock Ford was built in 1785, and was living there by 1793. The spacious four-story eighteenth century home overlooks the winding Conestoga River, and exists today in practically the same state as it did when one of the Continental Army's most famous generals lived there, now restored and opened to the public.

A New College is Named for Benjamin Franklin

The government warehouse on North Queen Street near James Street, unused after the Revolutionary War, became the second location of Franklin College, established in 1787.

Through the interest of two Lutheran and two Reformed clergymen, a movement to establish a college in Lancaster for the benefit of the German-speaking church groups in Pennsylvania led to the establishment of a liberal arts college in Lancaster, named for Benjamin Franklin, who was one of its first and most generous patrons.

On June 6th, 1787, distinguished trustees from Philadelphia and Lancaster assembled in the new Court House in the Square, and marched in a solemn procession to the new Trinity Lutheran Church, where the official dedication ceremonies took place. Following the dedication, the dignitaries met for a formal banquet, drinking toasts to the new nation and the new college, which was the third to be established in Pennsylvania. Four signers of the Declaration of Independence were members of its first Board of Trustees, as well as several future Governors of the Commonwealth and a number of distinguished jurists.

Franklin College started classes in a small stone building known as the "Brew House" but moved to larger quarters in the government building the following year. It did not remain a German college for any length of time, but had considerable difficulty until the merger with Marshall College in 1853 united the two colleges.

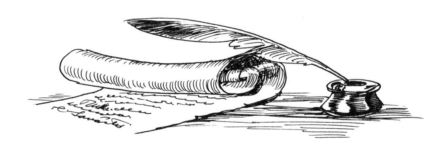

Moravians Begin a School for Girls at Lititz

The arrival of one small girl at the Sister's House of the Moravian community at Lititz in 1794 was the beginning of what was to become Linden Hall Seminary, the second oldest girl's school in the United States. The idea of having young girls live and board with the Moravian Sisters speedily developed into a school for training young ladies in culture and the arts, and providing a wholesome atmosphere for their education, and the school was eventually incorporated with an accredited course of liberal art studies.

The original buildings of the old Moravian community form part of its lovely campus and maintain much of the atmosphere of dignity and piety which were characteristic of its founders. Until 1863, it was known as the Lititz Boarding School, and was then incorporated as Linden Hall Seminary.

Picture from the Collection of Anthony R. Appel

Lancaster is the National Capital . . . for a Day!

The Congress of the United States had to keep moving during the darkest days of the Revolution, when Washington's army had to retreat from the Brandywine, and the capital at Philadelphia was threatened by the British invasion. The Congress decided that if it became necessary, they would move to Lancaster, the next largest town to the west, and when the legislators were hastily notified on September 19, 1777 that the enemy was near Philadelphia, they hastily departed by a round-about route, via Trenton, Easton, Bethlehem and Reading, finally arriving in Lancaster on September 27th. They took the Liberty Bell with them but a wagon break-down forced them to leave it on the way, and it was hidden in an Allentown church until the British threat to Philadelphia was ended.

It was an exciting time, as delegates and other refugees crowded into the town, and famous personalities like John Hancock, Samuel Adams, Richard Henry Lee and Charles Carroll assembled with the Congress, probably in the Court House, to conduct the nation's business. However, the chief business on that historic Saturday was the safety of the government, and after discussing routine business and means to supply General Washington with the necessary arms and supplies, they decided to keep moving to safer ground, and voted to place the broad Susquehanna River between themselves and the invaders, and move to York, which became the next national capital until the following July, 1778.

David Ramsay, Historian of the Revolution

Dr. David Ramsay, an active patriot and a surgeon during the Revolutionary War, was a native of Lancaster County. He was one of the first American historians, and wrote a history of the American Revolution, a history of the United States, and a biography of General Washington, who provided him with much information for his writings.

His birthplace was a little stone house in East Drumore Township, southern Lancaster County, where his Scotch-Irish parents had settled. Graduating from Princeton at the age of sixteen, young Ramsay studied medicine at the University of Pennsylvania, and practised medicine in South Carolina for a number of years, later becoming President of the Senate of South Carolina. When the Revolution broke out, Ramsay was banished to Florida by Lord Cornwallis, but later became a member of the Continental Congress.

His numerous histories were the first examples of a professional treatment of American history, and his writings are believed to be the first works for which a copyright was issued under the new United States government. He was shot by an insane person in 1815.

The Ramsay Monument at Unicorn

A Fireworks Display for President Adams

John Adams was the last President to occupy the national capital at Philadelphia, since Washington was to be the new capital after 1800. After the last session of the Congress at Philadelphia on May 14, 1800, President Adams planned to make a tour of the new capital site at Washington, and travelled by way of Lancaster and York. On May 28th, the second President of the United States arrived in Lancaster, taking lodgings at the *White Swan* Hotel in the square.

Some advance notice had been received about the President's visit, and a special display of fireworks was arranged in his honor that evening in the old prison yard at Prince and West King Streets. The next morning he journeyed to Columbia, escorted by a troop of volunteer cavalry, and took the ferry across the river, since no bridge existed at that time. Citizens and militia from York met him on the west shore and escorted him to York. President Adams commented that this was his second visit to Lancaster, since he had been present on September 27th, 1777, when Lancaster was the meeting place for the national government for one day during the Revolution.

The year 1800 was a bitterly contested election year, and political rivalry in Lancaster caused feelings to run high. Newspapers which opposed Adams and the Federalists took little notice of the President's visit.

George Washington Walks about the Town

"In the forenoon, I walked about the town," wrote George Washington in his diary on the Fourth of July, 1791, when the first President of the United States joined with the citizens of Lancaster in celebration of the national holiday.

Washington was making a trip through the southern and eastern states, and came to Lancaster from York on Sunday, July 3rd. His old Lancaster friend and military aide, General Edward Hand, went to Wright's Ferry to meet him, and with an escort of Lancaster citizens, the President's coach arrived at the outskirts of Lancaster about six o'clock that evening. At Abbeville, Washington left his coach and rode on horseback into the town, with church bells ringing, crowds cheering, flags waving, and the firing of cannon. He was entertained that night at the *White Swan* Hotel on the square, strolled through the streets of old Lancaster the next morning, and was formally entertained the rest of the day with an elaborate dinner in the Court House in the square. Fifteen toasts were presented, the final one to "The Illustrious President of the United States." After taking tea with General and Mrs. Hand that afternoon and spending a quiet evening with old friends, the President left Lancaster the next morning at four o'clock to go to Philadelphia.

Washington was no stranger to Lancaster, for he visited the town on three other occasions. He had visited in 1773, and dined here; he passed through Lancaster in 1794, returning from an inspection of troops involved in the Whiskey Rebellion; and in 1796 he spent the night here on his way from Philadelphia to Mount Vernon.

PART THREE: CITY AND COUNTRY LIFE

1800–1820

A Frenchman travelling through Lancaster in 1802 described the county farms as extremely fertile and filled with rich grain, as his stagecoach made numerous stops at roadside inns, where most of the conversation was in German. He found Lancaster to be a neatly planned town, with most of the dwellings made of brick, two stories high, and with churches for almost all denominations. The inhabitants he described as for the most part armourers, hatters, saddlers and coopers, and commented that the "armourers" had long been esteemed for the manufacture of rifle-barrelled guns.

The growth of the community led to its establishment as a city in 1818, and municipal problems began to receive more attention. Lotteries had been a common practise to raise funds for churches and community projects, and early street paving was financed by lottery tickets rather than by taxes. Space for a market had been provided for in the original Hamilton grant, and by 1800, a handsome brick building was erected on the square, serving as a "City Hall" in front, a site for twenty-four market-stalls in a connected structure, and above the market the headquarters of the Masonic Lodge. Fire protection was provided by several long-established volunteer fire companies, like the Union, Sun and Friendship companies, composed of many prominent citizens of the town. The city's water supply came entirely from dug wells and hand pumps on individual properties, and in 1810 a public well was dug near the court-house.

In the county, new townships and boroughs were being formed in increasing numbers, and county residents no longer had to come to the Court House in the square to cast their ballots at election time. After the lively national election of 1800 which resulted in the victory of the new Jeffersonian party, political rivalry became an important aspect of county life, and barbecues, caucus meetings and stump speeches in German and English were frequent and exciting occurrences.

European wars in the 1800's, and the subsequent War of 1812 had their effect on the community. A young Lancastrian, Robert Fulton, demonstrated his new invention of the submarine torpedo to both Napoleon and the British government, but returned to the United States to show its possibilities to his own country by blowing up a ship in New York Harbor. The constant threat of war had led to patriotic excitement, and even before war was declared in 1812, a volunteer militia unit, the "Lancaster Phalanx" offered its services to Governor Snyder. Later, when, the British invasion of Maryland took place, and Washington was burned, the Governor's call for emergency troops led to a citizens' meeting, and once again companies of volunteers from Lancaster County marched away to defend their new country.

The long years of international conflict brought about changes in both agriculture and industry. More wheat was being produced, to take the place of barley, and more than a hundred mills ground flour along the county's streams, to be carried to Philadelphia or Baltimore. Tobacco was beginning to be a profitable crop, and hempfields, the production of flax for linen textiles and the feeding of silkworms were common in the county.

Manufacturing was still in the home industry stage, and with the exception of a few large-scale enterprises like the charcoal iron furnaces, most manufactured products were made by skilled workers on their own farms or in their homes. Clock-makers, cabinet-makers, coopers, distillers, blacksmiths, coppersmiths, saddlers and wagonmakers found the agricultural wealth of the community to be a constant stimulus for their activities, and the increasing flow of travel through the area created constant demands for their products. But before long, canals and railroads were to enlarge the market area rapidly and the days of small home manufacturing would come to a gradual decline.

For more than a decade at the beginning of the nineteenth century, the capital of the Commonwealth of Pennsylvania was located in Lancaster, and all of the business of the state was transacted in Court House square area. The movement of the government from Philadelphia to Lancaster in 1799 was followed immediately by a bitter political campaign for the election of a governor to succeed Thomas Mifflin, who had served three terms as the first governor of the state. The new Jeffersonian Republican party nominated Thomas McKean, in opposition to a Federalist candidate from the western part of the state, James Ross. Chief Justice McKean was elected, but in general Lancaster County was Federalist in its sympathies, with most of the Republican opposition coming from the Scotch-Irish communities.

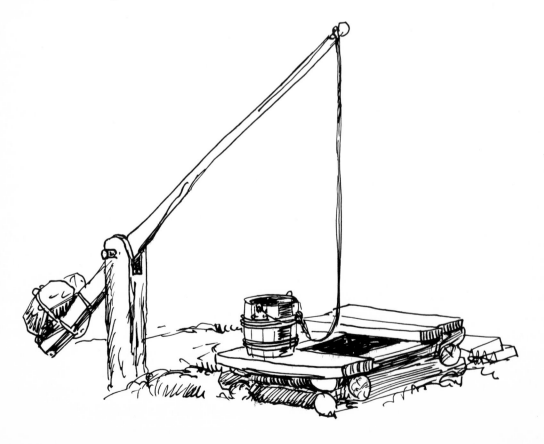

Lancaster Becomes the Capital of Pennsylvania

Lancaster was the capital of the Commonwealth on two occasions—first during the dark days of the Revolution, from October 1777 until June 1778, when Washington's army was at Valley Forge. The State government met in the Court House in the square, and despite the critical condition of the nation, they proclaimed December 18, 1777 as a day of Thanksgiving and praise.

During the 1790's, it was felt desirable to move the capital from Philadelphia to a more central location, due to the fear that the surroundings of a large eastern city would influence the legislature at the expense of rural western areas, and for several years, other cities were recommended, including Carlisle, Reading, Lancaster, Harrisburg and Wright's Ferry. After a deadlock over Harrisburg in 1799, Lancaster was chosen, and the State Legislature had its first meeting here on December 3, 1799.

Moving the official possessions of the government of Pennsylvania from Philadelphia to Lancaster was not a complicated or expensive project. The chairs, tables, desks, carpets and stoves were moved in two weeks, at a cost of one hundred and thirty-five dollars, and distributed in the available public buildings in Lancaster. The old city hall building in the square was probably used for executive offices, while the legislature used the new Court House building.

A short time after the government was established, inaugural ceremonies for a new Governor, Thomas McKean, took place, followed by an inaugural banquet and a torchlight procession by enthusiastic Republicans in the evening. McKean was sworn into office on December 17th, although at the last moment it was discovered that no arrangements had been made to have a qualified person administer the oath, and an express rider had to gallop to Salisbury Township for a judge.

The new Governor's first official act was the formal announcement of the death of General Washington, who had died on December 14, 1799.

In 1808, Simon Snyder, a native of Lancaster was elected Governor. In 1812, after many debates in the legislature about the merits of other Pennsylvania cities as possible capitals, the state government moved to Harrisburg.

Local officials were annoyed for some years because they claimed the State government had stolen the stove from the Lancaster Court House when the capital was moved from the town!

Punishment on the Pillory

Colonial laws were harsh when judged by modern standards, and criminals or law-breakers often were sentenced to severe physical punishment. A familiar object in most communities was the pillory, where the unfortunate wrong-doer was fastened by neck and wrists in the public square, to be ridiculed and sometimes abused by fellow-townsmen or mischievous pranksters.

Old Lancaster had its wooden pillory and a whipping post in the square until shortly before the Revolution, and records show that it was not just a decoration. On one occasion, a man accused of sedition against the King was sentenced to stand for an hour in the pillory, and to receive fifteen lashes on his bare back at the whipping post. Even women occasionally had to submit to such punishment, and a woman convicted of forgery in 1757 received the same sentence—an hour in the pillory and fifteen lashes on the bare back. Horse stealing took place frequently, but it was a serious offense and usually punished by a public whipping. It must be remembered that Lancaster County extended over a large area of almost 5,000 square miles at that time, and all county trials were held in this county seat. Consequently, many of the offenders were strangers to the community, and objects of special curiosity to local residents.

A Public Execution

Punishment of criminals was carried out publicly in old Lancaster. In 1821, a convicted murderer, John Lechler, was marched through the streets, escorted by militia companies, two cavalry troops and the City Band. At the gallows on the commons west of the city, fifteen thousand people came to witness the hanging, and made a public holiday out of the event.

The legend persisted that the unfortunate Lechler was so fond of marching with military units that he led the parade of military escorts with a brisk and enthusiastic step on his way to the scaffold.

Execution by hanging was not an unusual penalty in earlier years, and was often the penalty for burglary as well as for homicide. Women often were sentenced, but the penalty was usually changed to a term of imprisonment. During the year 1778, when the British occupied the eastern portion of Pennsylvania, all trials for murder, treason, manslaughter and similar offenses committed in Philadelphia, Bucks or Chester County, were tried in Lancaster courts by Lancaster juries.

Public punishment, whether on the scaffold or the pillory, was believed to provide a warning to everyone that crime does not pay. Counterfeiting was a fairly frequent offense, and one counterfeiter was sentenced to twenty lashes at the whipping post, and to have both of his ears cut off. Thieves were publicly whipped, and wore a large letter "T" on their coat for a period of six months. Even persons "who should be clamorous with their tongues" by shouting or scolding, could be sentenced to be gagged and made to stand in the pillory. Most of these punishments were associated with colonial laws, and removed in the early nineteenth century.

Citizens Serve on the Night Watch

In the absence of an organized police force, the duties of a citizen might also include service as a night watchman, to patrol the dark streets, keep watch for fires, and look out for suspicious activities during the night hours.

Suspicion of several acts of arson in 1810 caused the citizens to hold a town meeting and appoint a committee of sixteen men to act as a patrol, and to make a list of the borough residents for possible service. Persons unwilling to serve or unwilling to find a "decent man" as a substitute were to be fined one dollar for each night.

The volunteer patrolmen carried a lantern and a watchman's rattle to give warning of fire, and were authorized to arrest and jail vagrants, disorderly and suspicious persons who might be found in the streets at an unusual hour and who could not give a satisfactory account of themselves.

The volunteer fire companies were usually responsible for demands that regular night watchmen should be employed, because of the constant danger of fire from open fireplaces, blacksmith shops, candles, oil lamps, and rows of wooden buildings and stables.

"No Smoking" on the Streets!

Early ordinances of Lancaster prohibited smoking on the public streets, but one of the first violators was John Passmore, who became the first Mayor in 1818. He was the first man to be fined and cheerfully paid twenty shillings!

Help for Yellow Fever Victims in Philadelphia

The summer of 1793 brought a serious epidemic of Yellow Fever to Philadelphia, causing the death of about five thousand inhabitants. Accounts of the rapid spread of the plague and the helplessness of many citizens led General Edward Hand and other residents of Lancaster to appeal for contributions of food and supplies to be sent to the victims. Several hundred barrels of flour, more than a thousand dollars in cash and numerous packages of clothing were collected and delivered to Philadelphia.

The First Newspapers

As early as 1752, the first newspaper was published in Lancaster by Henry Miller and S. Holland. It was called the "Lancaster Gazette" and was a small, four-page paper published with both English and German columns.

When the State government moved to Lancaster in 1777, the "Pennsylvania Packet," an important Philadelphia newspaper, was printed here. Two major newspapers were started a few years later, the "Lancaster Journal" in 1794 and the Lancaster "Intelligencer" in 1799. The Journal was Federalist in sympathy, and the Intelligencer supported Jeffersonian Republicanism. In the bitter political battles of the early 1800's, newspaper editors indulged in violent and immoderate accusations, and for a short time, the editor of the Intelligencer, William Dickson, had to write his editorials in jail, where he languished as the result of a libel suit.

A Victory Dinner for Thomas Jefferson

The election of Jefferson in 1800 was the first time in United States history that a new party had gained control of the government, and the occasion was widely celebrated by Jeffersonians all over the county. On New Year's Day, 1801, a tremendous celebration was held in old Franklin College, on North Queen Street, with the presence of the Governor and most of the state officials, since Lancaster was the capital city. A volunteer infantry company assembled at the square and marched out to the banquet hall, where they fired volleys of musketry. A portrait of Jefferson hung behind the head table, and more than two hundred guests were seated in the three rooms which had been opened to form a large banquet hall.

The dinner lasted from two o'clock in the afternoon to six o'clock in the evening, with sixteen formal toasts, and almost the same number of "volunteer" toasts. In the evening, they paraded back through the town streets, preceded by a band and a tremendous lantern, seven feet high and five feet wide, called the "Temple of Liberty." It was a glorious day for the Jeffersonian Democrats, and a sad one for the defeated Federalists.

**William Henry's
Gun Factory**

Lancaster was an important center for arms manufacturing from colonial days until the Civil War, and one of the most prominent gun manufacturers was William Henry, gunsmith, inventor and statesman. Henry lived near the square from the 1740's until 1786, and for a time was in partnership with the wealthy Joseph Simon, Indian trader and merchant, who had a store in the square.

It is believed that a large stone building along Mill Creek was used by Henry for production of his rifles, when he began manufacturing on a large scale. He was Superintendent of Arms during the Revolution, and also had charge of providing leather goods for the army, and became well-known in the new national government, since he was also a delegate to the Continental Congress.

William Henry had been intensely interested in steam power, and visited James Watt in England in 1761 to study his work with steam engines. As early as 1763, Henry had built a steamboat to try out on the Conestoga River—an experiment that may have been the first trial of a steamboat. John Fitch, who successfully operated a steamboat in 1787, was frequently with Henry in Lancaster, and young Robert Fulton must have been familiar with the experiments in steamboat operation which the two inventors conducted on the Conestoga Creek.

Andrew Ellicott, Surveyor of the National Capital

When the new national government selected a site along the Potomac as the location for the new Capital in 1790, a French engineer, Major L'Enfant, who had come to America with Lafayette during the Revolution, was selected to plan the new city. It is not generally known that L'Enfant was discharged shortly after his appointment due to insubordination, and another engineer, Andrew Ellicott, did the actual work. L'Enfant refused to surrender his original plans, and Ellicott proceeded on the basis of his informal knowledge of the original ideas, and his own plans. L'Enfant had originally wanted $95,000 for his work, which Washington thought was only worth several thousand.

Ellicott plotted the latitude and longitude of the site, and laid out 1,146 blocks of streets, to conform to the broad avenues of the new city. His original map shows avenues of 130 to 160 feet wide, and streets from 90 to 110 feet wide.

Ellicott was a well-known engineer, who had surveyed part of the Mason-Dixon Line, the boundaries of Florida, and the boundaries of Pennsylvania and New York. When he was appointed Secretary of the Land Office of Pennsylvania, he moved to Lancaster, the State Capital, in 1801, and lived on North Prince and Marion Streets till 1812, when he became head of the new military Academy at West Point, and Professor of Mathematics.

Ellicott assisted Lewis, of the Lewis and Clark expedition, when Lewis came to Lancaster to secure arms for his party, in 1803, giving him advice about mapping, surveying and exploring the uncharted lands of the Louisiana Purchase.

The Evangelical Lutheran Church of the Holy Trinity

The magnificent spire of Trinity Lutheran Church on South Duke Street has been a distinctive landmark for many years, but the church had its beginnings many years before the present structure was completed in 1794. In 1729, while the county of Lancaster was being established, a travelling missionary, John Casper Stoever organized a congregation in old Hickorytown, and in succeeding years a number of church buildings were erected. A church built in 1734 was replaced on the present site with a new building in 1766, on which the bell tower and steeple eventually were placed by 1794.

Many significant events in Lancaster history are associated with Old Trinity Church. In 1771, the largest pipe organ in America was built for the church by David Tannenberg, of the Moravian community at Lititz. The church bell was cast in London and hung in the tall steeple years before the Revolution. One of its most famous pastors, Rev. G. H. E. Muhlenberg, also well known as a distinguished scholar and botanist, was deeply interested in education, and when Franklin College was established with ceremonies in Trinity Church in June, 1787, Rev. Muhlenberg was chosen as its first President.

Thomas Mifflin, first Governor of Pennsylvania, died in Lancaster when the city was state Capital, and was buried in Trinity churchyard. Thomas Wharton, Jr., President of Pennsylvania's early Executive Council also died here and was buried in the old church.

In the 1830's when the railroad line was brought into Lancaster from the north-west, engineers used the steeple of Trinity as a sighting point for their survey, and laid the tracks in a straight line from the main line to N. Queen and Chestnut Streets, in line with the tall spire.

The architecture of the Trinity steeple has been practically unchanged since 1794. The carved statues of the four evangelists, Matthew, Mark, Luke and John stand at the base of the tower, below the one hundred and ninety-five foot steeple.

Old Trinity Church

George Ross, Signer of the Declaration of Independence

One of the outstanding national statesmen from Lancaster was George Ross, who had settled in Lancaster in 1751, and was appointed Prosecutor for the Crown, under English rule. He became a leader of the patriots during Revolutionary days, was one of the signers of the Declaration of Independence, and a representative from Pennsylvania. Shortly afterwards he served as Vice-President of the Pennsylvania Constitutional Convention, with Franklin as President. The location of his home on Ross Street near Shippen is indicated by an historical marker.

Robert Fulton Invents a Better Steamboat

Robert Fulton, whose birthplace still stands in southern Lancaster County, spent much of his boyhood in the town of Lancaster, and developed an interest and talent for art and drawing while he was apprenticed to a jeweler. Old Lancaster was familiar to him through his teen-age years, as he came to know William Henry and the workmen of his gun-shop, watched the celebrations and fireworks during the war years, and saw early experiments with steamboats on the Conestoga River.

While Fulton became known nationally as the inventor of the first successful steamboat, the *Clermont,* his career resulted in many other significant achievements. Going to Philadelphia at the age of seventeen, he became an accomplished artist and portrait-painter, and in 1786 he went to London, spending several years studying art with Benjamin West. Engineering began to interest him more than art, and in London and Paris, he devoted considerable study to uses of steam power for navigation. He interested Napoleon in a submarine torpedo boat, and conducted experiments for the French government, remaining submerged in his new invention on one occasion for an hour, but the idea was too novel for the French at the time, and he was invited by the British to demonstrate the new method of undersea warfare. However, with tension growing between Great Britain and America, he returned to New York in 1806, and conducted a successful experiment with his torpedo in New York Harbor in 1807, completely destroying a brig.

The steamboat was still his major interest, and in the same year, after much public ridicule about "Fulton's Folly"—the *Clermont* amazed a skeptical public by making its way up the Hudson, and the great era of steam navigation revolutionized river transportation. Fulton married and made his home in New York until his death in 1815.

The George Ross House

The Robert Fulton House

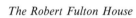

The Old Court House Burns

In June, 1784, the old Lancaster County Court House, which had stood in the center of the Square since 1739, was completely destroyed by fire, after having served the needs of the county and the community for forty-five years. It had been a two story brick building, with a clock-tower and cupola on top, a large brick-paved courtroom on the first floor and several meeting rooms above. The coat-of-arms of the King of Great Britain was painted above the judge's chair until the Revolution. The pillory, stocks and whipping-post stood outside in the square, which was often the site of a muddy duck-pond in wet weather. The old building was the scene of the important Indian Treaty of 1744, many cere-monies and banquets, and the meeting place of the Congress of the United States in 1777. Among its many functions was to serve as a dancing school for a time, but this offended some of the more serious inhabitants. It was also a storage house for powder during the French and Indian Wars.

The disastrous fire may have been caused by some slaked lime being used for repairs, or perhaps the repairman working on the clock at that time may have been responsible, but at any rate the destruction was complete. The court met at the home of Frederick Hubley until February, 1787, when the new Court House was completed on the same location, where it remained until 1854.

City Life Centers About the New Court House

The land on which the original Court House stood was given by Andrew Hamilton when the county was formed, and the first building was erected in 1739, serving many functions till it was destroyed by fire in 1784. A new Court House was completed in 1787 and remained there until 1854, during which period it was the scene for the inauguration of Franklin College, the visits of Washington, and many receptions to other notables, as well as an early nomination of James Buchanan for the Vice-Presidency.

The square served as a public market for many years, until a market house was provided, along with a City Hall on the north-west corner. Near the same corner was the residence of William Henry, gunsmith and pioneer in steamboat navigation. Across the square on the south-east corner was the famous *White Swan* Hotel, most prominent and famous of all the colonial inns, operated for many years by Matthias Slough, patriot and civic leader. On the south-west corner, Joseph Simon, merchant and Indian trader, operated one of the largest trading stores in the colony, and shipped goods to remote sections of the west for many years. On the north-east corner, the father of Robert Fulton, inventor of the first successful steamboat, operated a tailor shop, and young Robert played in the square as a boy, perhaps near the Henry gun shop. The *Conestoga Waggon* was formerly the *Grape* Tavern.

The Governor Calls for Volunteers in the War of 1812

A month before President Madison issued a proclamation of war against Great Britain in June, 1812, Governor Snyder of Pennsylvania called for the formation of volunteer militia regiments, and an organization of local citizens, the "Lancaster Phalanx" offered its services at once. Hostilities began along the Great Lakes and the first volunteers were not called out, but a year later the British fleet sailed up the Chesapeake Bay, threatening Baltimore and approaching Elkton, Maryland. Volunteers from nearby counties in Pennsylvania moved to the defense of Elkton on their own initiative, and the Lancaster Phalanx, almost one hundred men in number, marched to Maryland, joined on the way by the Pequea Rangers. The invasion danger passed, and the troops returned, with the thanks of the Governor of Pennsylvania, and the information that they would receive no pay for their services since they were outside the state limits.

A more serious danger developed the next year, in 1814, when the enemy captured the city of Washington and burned the capitol. Town criers read a proclamation by the Governor, calling for the assembly of five thousand militia at York for a movement to Baltimore. A short time later, Lancaster county troops were witnessing the bombardment of Fort McHenry, while a prisoner on a British war ship, Francis Scott Key, was writing the "Star-Spangled Banner."

Young James Buchanan made his first public speech in Lancaster, supporting the Governor's call, and volunteering to join the group of horsemen who rode to Maryland.

The war ended officially with the Treaty of Ghent on Christmas Eve, 1814, but the news did not reach the United States until February. Lancaster celebrated the peace with military parades and a ball at the *Red Lion* Tavern.

The First Bank

Although Lancaster was the second largest town in Pennsylvania in 1800, there were no banks in the community to protect the cash or furnish the credit involved in the many early commercial activities of its citizens. Merchants and traders kept their cash in strongboxes, loaned money to their friends and associates, and conducted their own banking activities until 1803, when a branch of the Bank of Pennsylvania was established at the north-east corner of West King and Prince Streets.

In 1810, citizens of the community established their own bank when they incorporated the Farmer's Bank of Lancaster, to "promote agricultural improvements, ex-tend domestic manufactures, and increase trade." The first bank was located at 41 North Queen Street, but in 1814 it moved to the corner of East King and South Duke Streets, aside of Miller's Hotel, and re-mained at that location until the present time. This is the oldest bank in the Lan-caster community.

It is interesting that during its early years, the scarcity of hard currency led to the printing of fractional paper currency, in denominations as low as five cents, ten cents or twenty cents. Since early printing was rather crude, there were several cases of counterfeiters who could easily reproduce the early banknotes.

Some Historic Churches

Presbyterians did not arrive in Pennsylvania in large numbers until the early 1700's, but when the migrations from Scotland and northern Ireland began to increase at that time, a small congregation was organized in Bart Township about 1727, and the Middle Octoraro church was supplied with a pastor every sixth Sunday. About the time of the Revolution, a sturdy stone church was erected, still standing on land secured from the Penn family for use of the congregation.

While a number of Mennonite meeting-houses were built by various congregations from the earliest years of Lancaster County, the old Mennonite church at Landisville, built about 1790, was very typical of the small log churches which spread over the country side, to replace the necessity of holding meetings in the homes of members.

The German Lutheran congregation in old Manheim became the special interest of "Baron" Stiegel, ironmaster and glass-manufacturer. When the original log church was to be replaced by a new building in 1772, Stiegel gave the congregation the deed to the land, with the romantic rental agreement of one red rose, payable to Stiegel and his heirs forever during the month of June each year. For many years the rental was ignored, until the tradition was re-established, and the "Feast of the Roses" has become an important community observance.

In the 1750's Jesuit missionaries organized a mission station in the Donegal area, and a log church was built by the St. Peter's congregation in 1768. In 1799, while the congregation was a mission church of St. Mary's Church in Lancaster, the present stone church was built. The first regular Catholic mission in Lancaster, St. Mary's, was established in 1741.

At about the same time that Moravian congregations were being formed in Lititz, a small congregation built a log church in Mount Joy Township, in the year 1740. Rev. Jacob Lischy was its first pastor and the church was dedicated in 1753.

The old stone church near Willow Street, south of Lancaster, is believed to be the first Methodist Episcopal church building in the country, erected in 1791. The Methodist movement was just beginning to spread through America during the Revolutionary period, and both Bishop Francis Asbury and Father Martin Boehm became actively interested in the establishment of congregations in the Lancaster area.

A Reception for the Marquis de Lafayette

When General Lafayette visited the United States in 1825, he was invited to Lancaster, and received one of the most impressive ceremonies in local history. Escorted into town by cavalry and infantry, who rode out to meet him at Slaymaker's Hotel near Salisbury, he passed through a great arch of flowers on King Street, and addressed veterans of the Revolutionary War who assembled to welcome him. His visit was marked by dinners, balls, visits to schools, and frequent toasts to the memory of war heroes. When Lafayette died some years later, Lancaster's public buildings were draped in black mourning for six months.

His Honor,
the First Mayor

The Borough of Lancaster was incorporated as the City of Lancaster on March 20, 1818, and Governor Snyder appointed John Passmore as the first Mayor of the City. Attorney Passmore had not only the impressive title of "Hizzonor," but he also had an impressive figure, for he is reputed to have weighed four hundred and eighty pounds. He lived at Orange and Shippen Streets, where a marker stands in front of the residence.

His tremendous size and weight caused many anecdotes about him, including the story that at the time of his death in 1827, there was no hearse large enough to carry the body, and the casket had to be carried on a wagon.

PART FOUR: TRADE AND TRANSPORTATION

1820–1840

A quarter century of war in Europe had ended by 1815, and the young American nation had found that it was no longer entirely dependent on foreign trade and manufacturing for its economic life. By 1820, domestic manufacturing had been stimulated tremendously by blockades and embargoes, American tariffs, new developments in transportation and the growth of a new market as western emigration increased. Fulton's steamboat had revolutionized river transportation and the Ohio and Mississippi Rivers had become the great freight routes from north to south, but the turnpikes and great Conestoga freight wagons were still the mainstay of east-west transport until the era of the New York, Pennsylvania and Maryland canal systems.

These were years when it was not uncommon for a hundred great wagons to pass through Lancaster on a single day, with the clatter of six great horses, the jingling of polished bells, and the shouting of veteran drivers, for the main road to the west was still through old Lancaster. But the opening of the Erie canal led many communities to plan their own canals, and in the 1830's the Conestoga Canal opened what seemed to be destined to become the greatest period in county history. Already famous for turnpike traffic, the canal traffic to west, south and north by way of the Susquehanna was expected to provide a tremendous market for the county's products from iron furnaces, forges, mills, distilleries, and fertile fields of grain.

A short time later, the construction of the Philadelphia, Lancaster and Columbia railroad opened another facility for the commerce of the region, and with road, river and rail routes, the county was assured a continuous contact with the trade of the nation.

The borough of Lancaster had been chartered as a city in 1818, with a population of about 8,000, and its streets showed the signs of the new prosperity, as old shops like Demuth's Tobacco Shop, the Heinitsh Apothecary Shop and the Steinman Hardware Store were now joined by new shops and stores, like the Hager Store, opened in 1821. Dry goods stores, printers, harness makers, tailors, watch and clock makers, jewelers and furniture stores appeared on the main streets of Lancaster and of growing county towns. Factories began to replace home manufacturing in several products, beginning with the Lancaster Cotton Factory founded by the joint enterprise of local citizens, and succeeded in following years by factories producing guns, farm machinery, furniture and locomotives.

Banking facilities became more important in a period of national investment and prosperity and a number of new banks provided credit for economic expansion. Municipal ordinances provided for pavement and street improvements, and the old wells and pumps were supplemented by a public water system, bringing piped water into the city by 1837. The prosperity of the county, stimulated by the improvements in transportation, was reflected in the development of amusements, cultural activities, and a number of private schools. Museums, theatrical entertainments, an occasional travelling circus and exhibitions of waxworks found enthusiastic audiences. In addition to the many schools provided by the German congregations for their denominations, a large number of academies, and a public school system were established by the interest of the English-speaking population.

Farmers in Lancaster county had grown a wide variety of agricultural products, but up to this time, grain had been the most important crop, and scores of mills along the county's streams ground flour for shipment to Philadelphia and Baltimore. But in this period, tobacco, which had been grown in small quantities for many years, became a more important crop when farmers found it could be grown by methods which did not exhaust the soil. By the 1840's, tobacco culture, tobacco barns and cigar manufacturing had begun to become a major characteristic of Lancaster County economy.

Domestic politics in the age of Jacksonian democracy awakened political party rivalry over questions of tariff policies, federal and state aid for internal improvements like turnpikes, canals and railroads, and national banking policies, and state and national candidates for office appeared in the county frequently, to be greeted by enthusiastic rallies from local supporters and jeers from the opposition. They were lively, exciting, optimistic days for Old Lancaster, as they were for all of the rapidly expanding county.

Mills Were the First Important Industry

Wherever early settlers made their homes and planted grain, there had to be nearby mills to grind it for feed and flour. With many streams flowing through Lancaster County, the situation was ideal for water-powered mills, and some of them were established as soon as the first permanent settlers arrived in the 1720's. Along the Chicques and the Pequea and the Octoraro and many other streams, log or stone or brick mills were built, with milldams and sluices and great wooden wheels, turning ponderous millstones and conveyors and screeners by a combination of great wooden shafts, wooden pulleys, wooden gears and a network of leather belts.

The mills were located along the streams, and the roads found their way to the mills. Corn, wheat and other grain were brought by wagon to the mill door, hoisted by barrel or bagful by a rope dangling from a high wooden pulley into one of the upper floors, from which the grain passed through various hoppers and conveyors, moving by gravity to trickle into the center of the great stones or "burrs." The millstones, often imported from France, were carefully grooved on each face in a geometrical pattern usually designed by the miller, and required occasional "sharpening" with a millpick when the grooves became worn. The gentle, flexible power of the water-driven wheel and the dampness of the stones produced "water-ground" corn meal of a quality that became an American tradition.

In days when barter took the place of cash, the miller usually took a regular percentage, or "toll" of the grain as payment, stored his grain or flour in the mill until he was ready to ship it by freight wagon to the city. The mills became important neighborhood centers, as constant arrivals of wagons waited for their grain to be ground, and farmers had an hour or two to exchange the news, feed and water their teams, and laugh, joke or play pranks until the long drive home.

Covered Bridges Were Sound and Dry

Covered bridges became a common sight over the many small streams, and even over the wide Susquehanna River for many years, but began to disappear rapidly after the coming of the automobile age. There has been much speculation as to why they were covered, but the most logical seems to have been the practical plan of preserving the wooden floor and timbers as long as possible. Many of the early covered bridges were toll bridges, and once the structure had been built, it was comparatively cheap to cover the sides and construct a shingle roof, which would guarantee longer life. Another reason may have been the fact that cattle or horses might have hesi-tated to cross an open structure, but would feel as secure entering a covered bridge as they might feel in entering a barn. Regardless of the purpose, there is no doubt that the long, dark covered structure provided a welcome opportunity for shelter from a storm, or a secluded spot for a romantic interlude. One of the most unusual covered bridges was the double-decked mile-long bridge of the Susquehanna River between Columbia and Wrightsville, burned in 1863. It was forty feet wide, with two tracks, provision for foot passengers and carriages, and had two tow-paths, one above the other, for canal traffic. A canal dam was built a short distance downstream.

Conestoga Wagons Carried the Nation's Freight

The great Conestoga wagons, or six-horse bell teams, were a distinct characteristic of the Lancaster County area, where all transport of freight to the east or west had to be overland. The special design and construction of these freight-carriers varied slightly as they were manufactured for different types of cargo, but their essential structure remained the same. The bed of the wagon was long and deep, with a pronounced slope toward the middle, to keep a jouncing cargo in the center instead of pressing against the ends. The white home-spun cover slanted outward in front and rear, supported by broad hickory hoops, giving the wagon the familiar bonnet-like silhouette that made it different from conventional straight-end wagons. The driver did not sit on a wagon seat, but rode on a "lazy-board," extending out from the left side of the wagon, where he could apply the hand-brake, or rode astride the wheel-horse. This was probably responsible for the American custom of steering vehicles on the left, and driving on the right side of the road. High rear wheels with broad iron tires helped easy movement on soft roads, while smaller front wheels were better for turning. Individually designed iron brackets, braces and hinges on various parts of the wagon added distinctive features to each vehicle.

The jingling of brightly polished clusters of brass bells on the harness was a prized accessory for every team, and it became a custom of wagoners to demand a set of horsebells from an unlucky teamster who had to be pulled out of the mire. Consequently, the arrival in town of a wagoner "with bells on" indicated a safe journey, and considerable embarrassment greeted the team which arrived without its chiming bells. Hence, the familiar promise, "I'll be there with bells on!"

Stage Coach Lines Provided Regular Transportation

Stage coaches carried passengers regularly through Lancaster on the main pike from Philadelphia through Lancaster, Harrisburg, Carlisle and Chambersburg. Stages left the *Red Lion* Inn three times a week, at half-past six in the morning for Harrisburg, at a fare of two dollars. The Dispatch Stage Line, operated by Matthias Slough of the *White Swan* Hotel, left the *Swan* at five in the morning, arriving at Philadelphia the same evening. Along the main stage roads, coaches stopped frequently at taverns to rest or change horses, and there were many opportunities to stop—someone has computed that there were sixty-two taverns in the sixty-one miles to Philadelphia along the King's Highway. Some of the best-known stage stops were at the *White Horse*

Inn, in Salisbury Township; the *Sign of the Stage,* at Paradise; and the *General Washington* in Elizabethtown.

The completion of the Lancaster-Philadelphia turnpike stimulated the growth of new stage lines after 1794. A four-horse stage left the *Fountain Inn* on South Queen Street every Monday, arriving in Philadelphia the next day, for a fare of three dollars, including fourteen pounds of baggage. A stage left twice a week from the *King of Prussia,* for Elizabethtown and Harrisburg. A two-day stage trip took passengers from Lancaster to York and Baltimore, at a rate of about five and a half cents per mile. On the whole, there was almost as much stage service available as is provided by modern bus lines.

Fast Driving on the Plank Roads

Early dirt roads often became impassible for wagons and carriages during rainy seasons, and plank roads were often built for long distances through swampy ground. Timber was plentiful, and heavy planks were laid on logs to make a smooth, fast road. In Lancaster a "Plank Road" Company built such a road out North Queen Street to Manheim, alongside the dirt road, and it became a popular racetrack for local horsemen. "Turnouts" had to be provided at various intervals to allow passage for approaching vehicles, but if wagons or carriages drove off the plank road, a few protruding planks made it easier for the wheels to get back on the roadway again.

While the narrow plank road and one-horse carriage were not ideal for making new racing records, the time of two minutes and forty seconds to the mile would have been considered a record worth a little boasting. A favorite form of competition was racing to the next turn-out point before an approaching carriage made it necessary to pull off the plank road and allow the other vehicle to pass.

The Canal Begins an Era of Water Transportation

With the coming of the canal era in the 1820's and 1830's, many of the plans to connect the Conestoga Creek with the Susquehanna River materialized successfully, and the Conestoga Navigation Company, chartered in 1825, completed a seventeen-mile canal with six locks from Reigart's Landing at the foot of East King Street to Safe Harbor. It was hoped the new canal system would give Lancaster all the advantages of a seaport town, and large quantities of freight, coal, lumber and grain were carried in the great boats instead of the Conestoga wagons.

A boat named the "Edward Coleman" made the first trip in 1825, but the canal company had many difficulties. Spring floods destroyed the canal dams from time to time, and ownership of the company changed hands frequently. In 1837, the canal was operated by the "Lancaster and Susquehanna Slackwater Navigation Company," which opened their new operation with a gala cruise down the canal, with the accompaniment of a band, a banquet, and, of course, numerous toasts to the success of the new venture.

The Railroad Comes into Lancaster

When the Philadelphia, Lancaster and Columbia Railroad was planned, the tracks would have passed north of the city, until a committee of citizens petitioned the legislature to run the line through the center of the city, at North Queen and Chestnut Streets. Surveyors sighted toward the spire of Trinity Lutheran Church, and brought the railroad into the city by 1834.

When the railroad was opened in March, the first cars were drawn by horses, but a few days later, the first locomotive made the trip, carrying the Governor of Pennsylvania and other distinguished guests, making the trip from Columbia to Lancaster in one hour. Two locomotives, called the "Lancaster" and the "Columbia" operated on the line, making the trip from Columbia to Philadelphia in eight hours, at a cost of fourteen dollars and sixty cents.

A Railroad to Paradise

The original settlement at Strasburg was on the old road from Philadelphia, and at the beginning of the railroad era, in 1832, it was natural to plan for a railroad, to continue the connection of the community with other transportation facilities. A charter was secured from the Pennsylvania legislature to construct a line connecting with the railroad at Leaman Place near Paradise, but although grading was completed, financial difficulties delayed completion of the project at that time. Some years later, the line was put in running order, and although financial problems continued from time to time, its restoration in recent years has given the Strasburg Railroad the reputation of America's oldest short-line railroad, and the claim to having been in business longer than every other railroad company in America with the exception of the Baltimore and Ohio.

Supplies of firewood and water had to be available along the line, and wandering cattle were always a hazard. Complaints about the danger of fires starting from sparks thrown from the engines were frequent from property owners along the railroad lines, and were often justified.

Abraham Witmer
Builds a Bridge

Even though the Philadelphia-Lancaster Turnpike was completed by 1794, no provision had been made for crossing the Conestoga River east of Lancaster except by fording the stream, and wagon and carriage traffic, including the members of the Continental Congress, had to cross through the water until a public spirited citizen named Abraham Witmer decided to build a bridge himself. His first structure was a wooden bridge, but by 1800 he had received permission from the legislature to construct a permanent bridge and charge toll. In November, 1800, a beautiful nine-arch stone bridge was opened to turnpike traffic, and an inscription stone was placed in the north wall reading, "This bridge was built by Abr. Witmer and Mary, His Wife, and completed in the year of our Lord, 1800." He operated the bridge privately until 1817, when the county secured a court order and took over the bridge, but refused to pay Witmer the assigned amount. It was poor treatment for his public-spirited action, and a poor reward for a fine old structure which remained in use for more than a hundred years.

This crossing of the Conestoga was part of the "King's Highway," laid out in 1733 by order of the Governor and Council of Pennsylvania, and running from the Court House through East Lampeter, Leacock and Salisbury townships, and on to Philadelphia. The colonial government made this a public highway by clearing the trees along a line of marked trees to a thirty-foot width, and clearing the underbrush on one side to a width of fifteen feet. The colony was supposed to provide necessary bridges, but the Conestoga River could usually be forded, and some years later, about 1777, Henry Dering built a stone tavern and ferry house on the bank of the stream, and provided ferry service for crossing at times of high water. The crossing was known as "Dering's Ford" for many years before Witmer's Bridge was built.

Before any bridges existed in America, settlers found shallow places where streams could be forded at normal water levels, and most of the old roads led to these fords. Even after bridges had been built, many travellers preferred to drive their teams through the water, stopping for a moment to give the horses a chance to drink. Using the ford might also save bridge toll, unless the water was too high.

Tavern signs, swinging overhead from iron brackets or mounted on posts in front of the old inns, were probably the most colorful aspect of old Lancaster streets. Following the old English custom, the taverns were named for animals or birds, like the *Bear,* the *Swan,* the *Golden Lamb,* or the *Bird-in-Hand;* or for famous persons like *William Pitt, General Wayne,* or the *King of Prussia;* or for almost any familiar object, like the *Conestoga Wagon,* the *Ship,* the *Fountain,* the *Bunch of Grapes,* or the *Rainbow.*

The traveller coming into Lancaster from Philadelphia about 1800 would have passed, on East King Street, such tavern signs as the *Indian Queen,* the *White Horse,* the *Black Bear,* the *State Arms,* the *General Washington,* the *Bull,* the *Ship,* the *Leopard* and the *Buck,* and from the center of town, would have been close to the *Indian King,* the *Red Lion,* the *Cross Keys,* and many others.

Changes in tavern ownership often brought changes in the name of the hostelry. When Adam Reigart left the historic *Grape* Tavern, the new owner called it the *Conestoga Waggon,* but the old name clung to it for many years.

Tavern Signs

An Interesting Tale

There is an interesting story about the sign of the *Three Crowns* tavern, in Salisbury Township, painted by Benjamin West. Patriots shot bullets at the three crowns on the sign, and the innkeeper painted *Waterloo Tavern* on the other side of the signboard, so that when British soldiers were in the vicinity, he could hide the bullet-riddled crowns, and display "Waterloo."

The White Swan

Most well-known of the old Lancaster inns was the *White Swan,* at the south-east corner of the square, operated for many years by Matthias Slough, whose father had built the hotel in 1754. Slough was prominent in both local and provincial affairs. He had been the county coroner at the age of twenty-one, and later became an assemblyman, and a colonel of Lancaster volunteers during the Revolutionary War.

The location of the *White Swan,* and the civic and political activities of Innkeeper Slough made his hotel a popular center for the entertainment of distinguished visitors, such as Washington, Lafayette, John Adams, von Steuben and many others. In the absence of the ball-rooms and banquet halls of modern hotels, the upper floors of hotels like the White Swan were frequently used for social affairs, formal dances, and civic ceremonies.

Matthias Slough operated the hotel from 1761 to 1806, and his family continued the operation until 1824. The name *Swan* was used by various inns, such as the *Black Swan,* the *Swan,* and the *Golden Swan.*

In addition to all of the distinguished statesmen who were entertained at the *Swan,* some of the guests were associated with unpleasant incidents. The proprietor found himself in charge of the horses of the Paxtang gang, when they rode into town, dismounted in his courtyard, and proceeded to massacre the Indians. On another occasion, in 1789, two prominent citizens became involved in an argument and fought a duel in his hotel, with fatal results for one duellist.

The Cat Tavern

During the Revolutionary War, many British and Hessian prisoners were held in Lancaster County barracks, far enough inland to prevent easy escape to the British lines. Officers of the troops who guarded them, under the command of General Moses Hazen, established the headquarters for their staff in the old stone *Cat* Tavern, located near Prince and James Streets, a short distance from the barracks.

The Plough Tavern

The old stone *Plough* Tavern, at the corner of King and Charlotte Streets, was one of the last of the original tavern buildings to remain unchanged until recent years. This was an important fork in the roads to the west, where the old Blue Rock Road branched off to the south from the road to Wright's Ferry. Blue Rock Road is now Manor Street, leading through Millersville. Lafayette and many other visiting dignitaries were entertained here during their stay in Lancaster.

The Red Lion Inn

The *Red Lion* tavern was built in 1812, in the first block of West King street, across from the old Steinman store. It became a social center of importance in the 1830's and its large ballroom was used as a theatre, with Joe Jefferson, famed actor, as its first attraction, in May, 1830. The *Red Lion* was a regular stagecoach stop for passengers en route from Philadelphia to Harrisburg on a schedule of three trips weekly.

Growing Mulberry Leaves for the Silkworms

Feeding silkworms on mulberry leaves to grow cocoons was a major industry in Lancaster for many years. Even before the Revolution, a Lancaster County woman was awarded a prize for raising the largest number of cocoons in Pennsylvania, and a silk mantle made from her product was presented to the Queen of England by Benjamin Franklin. As late as the 1840's, thousands of mulberry trees were being planted and cocooneries established in many places, but before long local silk mills were securing silk from China and local production ceased.

While Lancaster County led the entire state in silk production at the time of the Revolution, production declined until the 1830's, when the state offered a premium of twenty cents per pound. One of the large cocooneries on West Chestnut Street near Charlotte sent representatives to France to secure information and cuttings from the proper type of trees. Silk production involved hatching silkworms from eggs, feeding the worms on bits of mulberry leaves, waiting for the spinning of the cocoon, which took about one day and produced some four thousand yards of silk. The cocoons were dried, and the silk reeled off of the cocoon. Home manufactured silk handkerchiefs, stockings and other silk articles were common in the Lancaster county area. However, occasional damp spells in the climate, and the importation of many inferior grades of trees led to the decline of the industry.

One of the early problems in amateur production of silk was the difficulty of reeling the strands of silk from the cocoon, and recommendations had been made in Philadelphia before the Revolution that a public "filature" be established, where people could bring their cocoons and have the silk reeled off properly.

The Lancaster County Silk Growing Society, organized in 1839 at the *Leopard* Hotel, stimulated interest in many county towns. Columbia members planted about 30,000 mulberry trees, and sold buds at three cents each. The Warwick cocoonery near Manheim was awarded medals from the American Institute in New York for the quality of its cocoons.

Farmers in Manor township planted trees and erected large buildings to house the silkworms. Advertisements in county papers often offered silkworms and silkworm eggs for sale, but the boom finally expired and mulberry trees grew undisturbed throughout the county.

Lotteries Instead of Taxes for Street Improvement

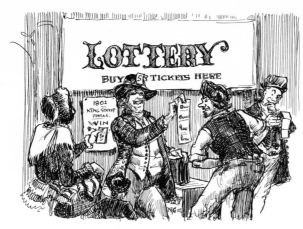

In 1792, the first turnpike in the United States was begun, between Philadelphia and Lancaster, and by 1794, a toll road with hard-surfaced tracks for wagon wheels had been completed, extending to the east end of Lancaster. Another turnpike company began constructing a road from the west end of Lancaster to the Susquehanna River, leaving a gap on this first hard highway to the west where it passed through the town, which at that time had the usual dirt roads, with deep muddy ruts in wet weather and clouds of dust the rest of the time.

Taxes would not have been popular to pay for paving the highway through the town, and the State legislature gave the town permission to raise $20,000 by holding a lottery. Thousands of tickets were placed on sale at three dollars each, with a first prize of $1000, a second prize of $500, and more than four thousand other prizes, some as low as $4.00. The needed money was easily raised when the drawing took place on May 1, 1802, and by May 28th, work began on paving the east section, from the Conestoga River to the Court House in the Square. Rock was blasted from nearby quarries, carts and wagons were hired, and within a few months the hard road through Lancaster matched the quality of the turnpike, and the managers of the lottery had made a nice profit for the community from the lottery.

Sidewalks Must be Paved with Brick

Among other municipal improvements after Lancaster became a city in 1818 was some attention to the condition of the sidewalks, which were usually either muddy paths or board walks. In 1823 a city ordinance was passed providing that after July 1st, all sidewalks had to be paved with brick.

The expenses of the new city were not very great, involving mostly pay for night watchmen, fuel and care for lamp-posts, fuel for heating the watchmen's shelters, painting street signs, and paving gutters. In 1846 the City Council considered changing the names of the principal streets from the English titles of nobility, such as King, Queen, Duke and Prince, to more democratic names, but no action was taken.

Volunteer Fire Companies Are Kept Busy

Volunteer fire companies, organized and manned by leading citizens, provided fire protection in early days, when insurance companies had not been organized, and when those who owned property had to protect it themselves by cooperation.

In Lancaster, the Union Company No. 1 and the Sun and Friendship companies were organized in the 1760's, and provided regulations for their members which included providing themselves with leather water-buckets, bags and baskets to remove valuables from burning houses, and assignments to various duties such as pumpers, ladder carriers, bucket-passers and hose-men. During the many years during which volunteer companies provided fire protec-tion, such notables as George Ross, Robert Fulton and James Buchanan ran with their companies to fight fires.

These volunteer fire companies encouraged many community improvements, such as street lighting, night watchmen, public pumps and community water systems. There was intense rivalry between different companies to see which group could arrive first at the scene of a fire, and occasionally there were lively disputes over the question of which company had the prior right to extinguish the fire. The purchase of a new engine for hand-pumping was the occasion for elaborate celebration, and handsome uniforms, parades and banquets became a part of the activities of the volunteer firemen.

Paper Currency for Small Change

little paper notes, in denominations of 10¢, 12½¢, 25¢ and 50¢, were called "shinplasters," and could be exchanged for a regular banknote when five dollars or more was accumulated. Some of the Lancaster notes had a locomotive on one side and an anvil on the other.

During the financial panic of 1837, when money became scarce all over the country, some Lancaster banks issued their own small currency to be used as change. The

Harvesting Grain

Harvesting of grain by sickle, scythe and cradle scythe had been the normal procedure by farmers and farm families for centuries, until the 1830's and '40's brought new inventions into use, to take advantage of the large areas of cheap fertile land that made large scale farming possible. Lancaster county inventors and manufacturers were among the many Americans who became interested in the possibilities of farming by machinery. One resident invented a threshing machine powered by horses which could produce five hundred bushels of wheat per day. A Clay township agent introduced the first McCormick reaper in 1851. Reapers were being manufactured at Mt. Joy and Brunnerville. One enthusiastic Democratic farmer produced a type of seed corn which he proudly christened "Buchanan Corn," because "it couldn't be beat!"

The Gap Nickel Mines

As early as 1730, valuable mineral deposits of copper were being mined near Gap, on a large tract of land which became known as the "Gap Copper Mines." At about the time of the Revolution, chemical springs were discovered in the excavations, which, it was claimed, had been examined by Benjamin Franklin and said to contain very rich deposits of copper.

In 1852, new operation of the mine revealed that much of the refuse ore which had been discarded contained large quantities of nickel, and the mines became the "Gap Nickel Mines." By the time of the Civil War, the Nickel Mines became a large and prosperous mining operation, employing more than a hundred men and erecting a company town as part of the operation. For a time this was the only nickel mine operated in the United States, but later discoveries of rich deposits in Canada led to abandonment of the project.

There were other mineral deposits in the county, responsible for many different mining ventures. Chrome deposits were discovered by a strange incident in 1827, when stones supporting a cider barrel in a market were identified as containing chromite, and led to the subsequent discovery of large supplies of the mineral near the Octoraro Creek. The Wood mine supplied most of the world's chromite until after the Civil War. Iron ore was mined in many areas of the county, such as the Grubb mine at Silver Spring, and other deposits near Marietta and Quarryville. Deposits of silver, lead and zinc were found and mined in lesser quantities but could not compete with larger deposits found in the west.

The original operation of the old copper mine at Gap involved the removal of water from the surface of the ore. Old residents testified to the peculiar qualities of the water, which would leave a heavy deposit of copper on a knife which was immersed in it for a short period, and iron bars collected large deposits.

Pumping the water out economically presented the alternatives of using a waterwheel to operate the pumps, or using a steam engine. After considering the difficulties of using steam power, such as the "high consumption of fuel, the frequent repairs, and the high wages which would have to be paid to the engineer," the pumps were operated by water power. The owners anticipated the production of three hundred tons of copper annually, at a value of $400 per ton, which would have meant receipts of $120,000 in 1797.

Cross Keys Becomes Intercourse

A small settlement at a crossroads about twelve miles east of Lancaster was the site of the old *Cross Keys* Tavern, built about 1754. The little village was called Cross Keys until 1814, when a land speculator laid out town lots and gave the settlement the name of Intercourse.

The "Old Philadelphia Road," which ran from Lancaster through Leacock township, passed by the old *Cross Keys* tavern and intersected a north-south road. When forty-eight acres of land were laid out into a hundred and fifty-one lots, a lottery was held by the promoter, distributing lots at $250 each. There were only five houses, including the tavern, in the settlement at the time, and even the announcement of the new name of "Intercourse" for the new town did not stimulate building for many years. However, its location at a busy cross-roads led to the establishment of other taverns and general stores by the middle of the century.

Kirk's Mills

At the extreme southern end of Lancaster County is one of the earliest settlements of the region, located along an old road that originally ran from Market Street in Philadelphia to the Susquehanna. Built in the mid-eighteenth century, Kirk's Mills still retains some of its original character, for the rebuilt mill, constructed in 1797 still stands along the millstream, and the miller's house nearby represents much of the original architecture in the interior. A small village grew in the vicinity, with a post-office established in the store.

After two hundred years, little remains today of the busy little village but its original buildings, almost hidden in the wooded valley. Much of the original character of their early construction can still be seen in the type of soft Swedish brick, made from an ancient formula, and still providing sturdy walls for the old mill, and in the log structure of one of the original buildings, where one wall remains exposed as it was constructed in 1760.

The road through Kirk's Mills was called "Street Road," and was surveyed through to McCall's Ferry at the time a bridge was being planned.

The Iron Industry at Martic Forge

Martic Forge and nearby Martic Furnace were the second iron manufacturing industries in Lancaster County, built about 1750 by Thomas and William Smith. The business remained active through the Revolution and for a number of years afterwards, and was eventually acquired by the Coleman family, wealthy Lancaster ironmasters. Ample supplies of bog iron ore were available in this part of southern Lancaster county, as well as plenty of limestone and hundreds of acres of timber for making charcoal.

Martic Furnace was built first, and Martic Forge was constructed about four miles away. The furnace went out of operation about the time of the Revolution, but the Martic Iron Company continued operations, with considerable financial difficulty, until 1872. Like many of the early iron industries, ownership of the company was divided many times among many different owners, one of whom was Edward Brien, who had married General Edward Hand's daughter.

The manufacture of cast-iron stove plates was one of the important operations of these early furnaces, and elaborate decorations and designs molded into the large flat iron plates were artistic examples of the individuality of each ironmaster or of his workmen. Five flat iron plates bolted together formed an iron box known as a five-plate stove, used for heating rooms more efficiently than the open fireplace, and ten plates produced a ten-plate stove, containing a compartment for keeping food or dishes warm.

The furnace produced "pigs" of cast iron as well as other cast iron products, and at the forge, the pigs were heated, hammered, rolled or slit into various shapes and sizes, such as iron bars or rods or strips. Water power was necessary for both operations, to operate a giant bellows for the air blast, or to raise and drop the great trip hammers at the forge, which could be heard clanging and thudding over miles of the countryside when the forge was working.

By the 1840's, most of the charcoal iron furnaces were being replaced by better methods, and most of them have become abandoned ruins.

Windsor Forge

Windsor Forge was built in 1742, on a large tract of land a short distance from Churchtown. It came into the hands of the Jenkins family, and developed into a typical ironmaster's estate during the next hundred years. The original forge and associated buildings no longer exist, but the mansion house, which served as headquarters for the owner of the estate still remains a characteristic example of the almost feudal relationship which existed between the ironmaster and the scores of workmen whose whole life was devoted to the operations of the forge, and dependent on the owner for their livelihood.

Windsor Forge was another example of an iron industry operated by a number of partners. It was built about 1743, on land originally owned by the Jenkins family, sold by them to an ironmaster, and later acquired again by the Jenkins family, who built the magnificent ironmaster's home known as the Windsor Mansion. It was later owned by Dr. John W. Nevin, who became President of Franklin and Marshall College, and who had married one of the Jenkins family.

The Caernarvon area had been originally settled by Welsh emigrants, and many wealthy ironmasters were associated with its iron industries. Cannon and ammunition were produced here in large quantities during both the War of Revolution and the War of 1812.

The Cattle Market at Blue Ball

The early settlement at Blue Ball, founded about 1760 at a crossroads tavern in eastern Lancaster County, became one of the most active and well-known cattle markets in the east for almost a century. In the 1790's, after western lands were drawing pioneer settlers from the new nation, a cattle trading business was started to furnish cattle and horses for the emigrants passing through to establish new homes in the west. It is not generally realized that in the years before the opening of the Far West, almost all cattle moved from the east to the west, and the best markets for eastern cattle were along the roads leading to the new lands. Drovers often spent many weeks on the roads bringing slow-moving herds of cattle to the market, gentlemen bought or traded horses, and gamblers speculated or outwitted innocent buyers. The *"Sign of the Blue Ball"* tavern became the headquarters for an immense amount of activity until many years after the Civil War. Early in the twentieth century a disastrous fire wiped out the cattleyards, and the trade was never resumed.

Demuth's Tobacco Shop: 1770

The Oldest Tobacco Shop in the United States

Still operated by the same family and on the original location on East King Street is the Demuth Tobacco Shop, established in 1770 to manufacture and sell snuff and cigars. For almost two hundred years, through the days of the Revolution, the Civil War and the twentieth century, famous residents and distinguished visitors have stopped at the historic spot to fill snuffboxes or procure tobacco. Its products were used by members of the Continental Congress, the State Legislature of Pennsylvania, when their official residence was in Lancaster, and by President James Buchanan.

The tavern sign of the nearby *William Pitt* tavern was painted by the noted artist, Jacob Eicholtz.

East King Street about 1800

Barr Builds an Ark

In southern Lancaster county, the quarrying of limestone became an important activity, after one of the early settlers, Martin Barr, acquired several thousand acres of land, and built a massive stone house on a hill. Local residents gave the prominent building the nickname of "The Ark" on "Mt. Ararat," and the house became a familiar landmark.

The foundation was sunk to solid rock, and the stone walls were two feet thick, and it was said to contain more stone than any other building in the county.

After the foundation and part of the house had been constructed, the owner was disappointed in the appearance of the gray stone, and completed the building with masonry stone of a different color.

The "Ark" was built during the years from 1790 to 1793, with interior woodwork of walnut, entirely fitted with wood pegs and pins instead of nails. The house was sixty-five feet long and fifty-five feet wide, with a large hallway through the center and a winding stairway to the top floor.

Barr's quarries provided many tons of lime for Lancaster and nearby counties. Naturally, the numerous quarries in the vicinity gave the growing community the name of Quarryville.

Professor John Wise Makes Another Balloon Ascension

One of the nation's first aeronauts was John Wise of Lancaster, who combined public exhibitions and stunts with serious scientific studies of the upper atmosphere in his balloon ascensions. From the 1830's through the Civil War years "Professor" Wise was making regular balloon trips from Lancaster and many Pennsylvania communities, dropping newspapers, parachuting small animals, and often making "parachute" descents himself by ripping his balloon apart.

He disappeared from sight in 1879, when he and two companions sailed over Lake Michigan, on what was to be his last flight.

Lumber Rafts Came to the River Towns

The movement of great rafts of lumber down the Susquehanna River in mid-century brought business activity and adventure to Marietta and Columbia, prominent centers of the lumber trade for many years. The sale of timber from cleared lands on the upper Susquehanna made the process of floating logs down river a profitable venture, at first for individuals and later for large logging companies. Great rafts were formed at the beginning of the spring season, when the water was high, and sometimes floated three hundred miles, to reach their destination.

PART FIVE: THE COUNTY IN MID-CENTURY
1840–1865

In the years just before the Civil War, many of the physical aspects of Old Lancaster had begun to change, and a few symbols of the coming age of industrialization were appearing. Although most manufacturing was still in homes and small shops, new factories, foundries and machine shops were appearing in the city and throughout the county, producing locomotives, boilers, water wheels and agricultural machinery. Agriculture dominated the county's industry, and its large grain production was responsible for more than two hundred grist mills. Throughout the county, foundries and shops had begun to produce reapers, threshers, plows and farm tools which found a ready market.

In Lancaster City, new buildings and institutions changed old landmarks, as a new Court House, an opera house, a new jail, a new college, a new reservoir and a new market house were constructed. An active cultural interest was expressed by the raising of funds through a community campaign to bring Marshall College to Lancaster to join with old Franklin College; the opening of the Fulton Opera House, which brought some of the finest drama and most notable musicians of the country to its stage; the opening of a college for prospective teachers at Millersville; and the organization of a number of societies, concerned with the study of natural science, literature or philanthropic affairs.

State and national political affairs began to have special significance for the city and county through the growing influence of two Lancaster citizens, Thaddeus Stevens, stern Whig and Republican, and dignified James Buchanan, Democrat and diplomat. As tension between free and slave states increased in the 1850's, the location of Lancaster County on the border of Maryland, a slave-holding state, made southern Lancaster County a natural path for escaping fugitive slaves, and the "underground railroad" had many "stations" in county barns or cellars, where runaways were illegally sheltered on their journey toward freedom. The riot at Christiana in 1851 was one of the first cases of citizen's protest against the unpopular Fugitive Slave Law.

The coming of the Civil War produced thousands of volunteers in Pennsylvania, and Lancaster County sent gaily uniformed local companies to Harrisburg and Washington in the first weeks of the war. The county escaped the storm of battle, but in the Gettysburg Campaign of 1863, it narrowly escaped invasion through the burning of the bridge over the Susquehanna River by militia companies, an event that stopped the successful march of Lee's army, and brought about a great battle further west at Gettysburg. The passage of large numbers of volunteer troops through Lancaster led to the early formation of women's groups like the Patriot Daughters, who provided food, clothing and medical supplies for the soldiers, and travelled to

Gettysburg to nurse the wounded. Raising funds by fairs and auctions, they were largely responsible for the Soldiers' and Sailors' Monument erected in the Square in 1874, in an area that had been empty for twenty years, since the Court House had been removed.

Although the war had provided a lively stimulus to the economic life of the community, through contracts for rifles, leather equipment, textiles, and the demands for minerals and grain, the life of the county was still predominantly influenced by its agricultural wealth. Annual or semi-annual fairs were major events of interest for every locality, providing entertainment and recreation as well as opportunity for the exhibition of agricultural products. Market-houses and curb markets were almost universally used for the purchase of foods, meat and vegetables. Efficient use of the fertile Lancaster County limestone soil by generations of descendants of pioneer settlers had led to a rich variety of agricultural produce which was later to justify the county's claim to the title "Garden Spot of America."

By mid-century, it had become apparent that the rare combination of pioneer industry, early trade and commerce, and constant agricultural progress, for a period of almost one hundred and fifty years, would assure the continued prosperity and progress of the Lancaster County area as it approached the challenges of the industrial age. The history of its people, from the days of William Penn, had provided Lancaster with a rich heritage which was typical of the American story.

The Old Jail

As the population of early Lancaster County grew, a county jail for debtors and other miscreants was built in the borough, at the corner of W. King and N. Prince Streets. It was built in 1740, constructed of sturdy logs, and with numerous additions and repairs, the installation of a well and pump, and the erection of masonry walls, served its purpose until 1774. At that time, due to frequent escapes and an increasing number of "guests," an entirely new stone building was built on the same site, including the old workhouse area. This prison, familiarly called "Old Eleven Steps" because of the entrance stairs on Water Street, remained in use until 1852. This old jail was the scene of the massacre of Conestoga Indians by the Paxtang Boys in 1763. Part of the original stone wall still remains below the Fulton Opera House.

The new jail, completed in 1851 on East King St., near the Reservoir, was as unusual as it was imposing. It was almost an exact model of old Lancaster Castle in Lancaster, England, with an arched gateway, portcullis, embrasured battlements, and a great medieval watch-tower more than a hundred feet high. Although some of its towers and battlements have been altered through the years, it has remained for more than a century as a distinctive landmark.

The New Jail

Fulton Hall Becomes an Opera House

Fulton Hall, the opera house built in 1852 on the site of the old jail, was an important center for civic affairs, social gatherings and entertainment for more than a century. Ole Bull, the great Norwegian violinist, was one of many notables who appeared on its stage. Here Lancaster audiences saw and heard Adelina Patti, Joe Jefferson, John Wilkes Booth, Buffalo Bill, Wild Bill Hickock, Sarah Bernhardt, Woodrow Wilson, Nazimova, and almost every great name in nineteenth century theatrical history.

Known as "Fulton Hall" in the years from 1852 to 1873, the building was the scene of college commencement ceremonies, public meetings, occasional sessions of court, military ceremonies and very elegant balls and concerts. In 1873, when the Hall had passed from the original association of business men into private hands, plans were made for its transformation into a formal theatre instead of a hall, and the "Fulton Opera House" came into existence.

The opening of the new theatre was a thrilling occasion for more than a thousand persons who attended a benefit performance of Shakespeare's "Othello," to raise funds for Civil War widows and orphans. One of the prominent actors of the age who appeared on the new stage at this performance called the theatre "the most beautiful temple of art in the United States."

James Buchanan purchased a beautiful country estate known as Wheatland in 1848 and used it as his residence until his death there in 1868. Here he and his beautiful niece, Miss Harriet Lane, received the news of his election to the Presidency in 1856, and he returned to this restful mansion in 1861, where he remained during the years of the Civil War. Buchanan was the nation's only bachelor President, and his young niece presided over the White House as the First Lady of the Land during his administration.

James Buchanan is Elected to the Presidency

James Buchanan, who became the 15th President of the United States, came to Lancaster in 1809 as a young law student and became a successful and wealthy lawyer. His career in politics made him one of the most experienced statesmen to enter the White House, for he had served as state legislator, Congressman, Senator, minister to Russia and Great Britain, and Secretary of State. His home at Wheatland became the scene of many state and social occasions, and citizens of Lancaster escorted him from Wheatland to the railroad station when he left for his inauguration.

Wheatland was an imposing mansion, with a square central portion, flanked by two wings. The house had some of the characteristics of the old South, with a central hallway from front to rear, and a long porch at the rear making an ideal spot for his quiet relaxation or informal meetings.

When the news that the distinguished Lancaster lawyer and statesman had been nominated for the Presidency on the Democratic ticket in June, 1856, citizens assembled at the telegraph office dashed in a mad scramble out to Wheatland to carry the news. Students from Franklin and Marshall College, excited because Buchanan was President of their Board of Trustees joined in the race, and were the first to reach Wheatland, where the candidate made a brief speech to the crowd of his fellow-citizens.

Buchanan retired to Wheatland after his critical years in the White House, and spent his remaining years in quiet enjoyment of the peaceful grounds and pleasant shaded lawns of his Lancaster home overlooking the wheatfields that gave it its name.

Rear Porch at Wheatland

Barns were Stations on the Underground Railroad

In the decades before the Civil War, runaway slaves from slave-holding states below the Pennsylvania border in southern Lancaster County often found friendly sympathizers who would hide the runaways in barns or cellars until it was possible to arrange to help them to move further north to freedom. The succession of willing friends along the escape route led to the name "Underground Railroad" for the "stations" along the way, where the runaway could hide. Many found their way into Lancaster County along the Susquehanna River to the river towns, and some made their way through the wooded areas in the south and east. The act of aiding a fugitive slave was illegal, but many Pennsylvanians felt that the law was immoral and need not be obeyed.

In the old Lancaster County barn pictured here, and many others like it, a hideaway was constructed under the sloping driveway into the barn, where several slaves could hide safely even if the property was searched by a slave-owner and officers of the law. Neighbors could not always be trusted and the utmost secrecy was maintained. Large rewards for information leading to the arrest of runaway slaves was a temptation which many could not resist.

Travel on the "Underground Railroad" was not always secret and peaceful. In a number of cases before the violent Christiana riot in 1851, residents of the county were enraged by search of their homes and seizure of slaves by slave-hunters without warrants or other legal authority. On other occasions, freed Negroes or runaways attacked the hunters willing to risk death rather than capture.

Donegal Presbyterian Church

Donegal Church was the home of one of the first Presbyterian congregations in the country, organized about 1721. The historic Witness Tree, scene of Revolutionary allegiance, is more than three hundred years old.

Making Wooden Pumps at Reamstown

In early days, when wells and pumps provided the only water supply, the manufacture of wood pumps to be installed in the shallow wells was an important occupation for carpenters or wood-workers. The stock, or pipe, extending down twenty or twenty-five feet into the well, was made of hollowed wood sections, tapered to fit tightly at the joints, and becoming airtight and watertight as the dampness swelled the wood.

The pump itself was a simple mechanism, consisting of a wooden valve container, shaped like a cylinder, and giving these pumps the name of "cucumber" pumps. A small wood-and-leather clapper valve created the necessary vacuum to draw the water to the top as the wood or iron handle was operated.

Reamstown, originally named "Zoar," was one of the earliest settlements of the county, established by Everhard Ream in 1723. The beginnings of this settlement seem typical of all the pioneer communities in America, for Ream came into this wilderness territory when the only inhabitants were Indians, stopped his wagon and team under a large oak tree, unloaded his belongings, and lived beneath its branches until he could construct a crude log house for his family. Descendants of the same family still reside in the area.

John Miller's Town Becomes Millersville

Like many early towns, Millersville had its beginnings when an ambitious settler decided to buy some land, distribute lots by a lottery and lay out a town.

While there were early pioneers in this old Indian territory in the early 1700's, it was not till 1764 that a Lancaster blacksmith named John Miller planned the community that was to carry his name.

The village remained a tiny settlement until the 1850's, when a local schoolmaster and other citizens planned a school to train teachers and established an academy called the Lancaster County Normal School. In 1857, the state legislature passed a normal school law, and the Millersville school became the first State teacher training school. Its picturesque old Main Building has been a distinctive landmark for many years, and the rapid growth of the college speedily changed the little rural community into a busy "college town."

Lampeter was not Named for "Lame Peter!"

Lampeter, one of the original townships of the county, had a number of Welsh settlers, and the area was named for Lampeter, in Wales, which took its name from St. Peter's Church. However, a long time ago, a resident wrote a fictitious novel in which he suggested that the name had come from a lame tavern-keeper named Peter Yeordy, and the legend persisted for many years.

One well-known native of Lampeter was the eccentric "Devil Dave" Miller, sheriff of the county in 1834, who was proprietor of the Washington House on East King Street. Part of his claim to notoriety came from one occasion when he delivered a legal paper to the judge by riding his horse into the Court House, up the steps and into the courtroom, where he dismounted and presented his documents!

Lampeter Township was one of the first areas in the county to be settled, when groups of Swiss Mennonites came from the Palatinate and Swiss Cantons in 1709 to establish their new homes in its fertile hills and valleys.

Tons of Epsom Salts

Among the many little-known resources of Old Lancaster were large deposits of magnesium sulphate, commonly known as Epsom salts, in the Oak Hill area of southern Lancaster County. In the mid-nineteenth century it was estimated that almost two million pounds per year were manufactured from mineral deposits along the high ridge of hills.

New Holland

The great emigration from Palatine Germany in the early 1700's led many settlers to fertile lands in eastern Lancaster, and in the area that became New Holland, a settler named Diffenderfer seems to have been the leader of the first party of pioneers. The little group set up a Lutheran congregation and church shortly after settlement, although the name of New Holland was not adopted until the time of the Revolution. The town developed along one long street with several angles, giving rise to the doubtful legend that it had originally been a wandering cattlepath, but it was probably an Indian trail, which later became the Horseshoe Road.

One of the first settlers in the eastern part of Lancaster County was a Swiss emigrant who had arrived in Pennsylvania as early as 1696, and is believed to have found his way into the Earl township area in 1717, looking for stray horses. Hans Graaf and some of the early German emigrants settled in the area, where Graaf bought a large amount of land, built a mill on a small stream which became known as Graaf's (or Groff's) Run, and when a township was formed in 1729, it was named Earl, which was the English equivalent of the German word "Graf," a title of minor nobility.

Groffdale

Graaf became a prominent citizen of the new settlement, and when the King's Highway from Philadelphia to Lancaster was being laid out in 1733, he was placed in charge of some of the work.

Boat-Building at Elizabethtown

Like many colonial towns, Elizabethtown had its beginnings when an enterprising trader set up a cross-roads tavern and trading post in 1735. Travel and trade along the old road toward Paxtang and the Susquehanna River caused the settlement to grow and the *"Bear"* tavern became its most historic landmark.

In later years, when the era of canal-building brought water transportation at cheap rates to many portions of Pennsylvania, craftsmen in Elizabethtown took to the construction of great canal-boats. They were built for canal and river use, and launched on the Conewago Creek, to carry great quantities of freight to the south or west on the new waterways.

"Malt Capital of the Nation"

In an area which produced as much grain as the Lancaster County area, the malting of grain became an important industry in many of the county towns. For a time, one of the malt houses in Mount Joy claimed the title of the "Malt Capital of the Nation," but many other malt houses might have disputed the claim. In the Moravian community of Lititz, church authorities encouraged the malting of grain for a time, hoping that increased production of beer would discourage the growing consumption of distilled liquor.

Distilleries were numerous in this grain

country, and in the 1830's, their number surpassed the number of grist mills—there were one hundred and sixty-four grist mills, and one hundred and eighty-three distilleries listed—to say nothing of an additional number in remote sections which were not listed.

Mount Joy, settled in 1811 by Scotch-Irish emigrants, is believed to have been named for an historic rescue ship, the *Mountjoy,* which saved besieged citizens of Londonderry, Ireland, in 1699, by crashing a river barricade and bringing supplies to the starving Scotch-Irish inhabitants.

In the early days of the nation, the arrival of a "Circus," a menagerie, or a travelling magician, was an event causing much community interest and excitement. Crowds came to the *Sign of the Lion* on North Queen St., to see the "Learned Pig," which, it was claimed, could read printing and writing, in English and German, could spell, could tell the time of day, and could subtract and multiply!

A camel, a lion or an elephant would occasionally be brought to a tavern courtyard as a special attraction, or be displayed in town during the fair season.

Entertainment: From Pigs to Pictures

For evening entertainment, the Lancaster Museum provided a wide variety of curiosities, wild animals, waxed figures, and occasionally a magic lantern show, called by the exciting title of "Phantasmagoria!"

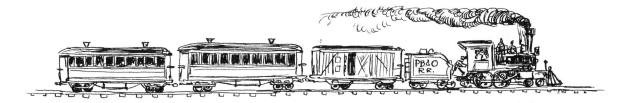

The Narrow-gauge Peach Bottom Railroad

A small narrow-gauge railroad winding through the hills from Oxford and along the Octoraro Creek in southern Lancaster County to Peach Bottom was typical of many short-line (and short-lived) railroads constructed in the mid-nineteenth century, mainly to serve local needs. Small business with farm produce, flour, tanned leather or sawmill products found that unless they could ship by rail, they could not meet the competition of other industries located along main railroad lines.

The Lancaster, Oxford and Southern Railroad, became known successively as the "L.O.&S.," the "Little, Old and Slow," and finally simply as "Peachy." Its tracks were three feet, six inches wide, about a foot narrower than the standard gauge tracks and its original surveyors planned a low grade line which avoided steep hills, so

that the tracks wandered along the creeks until they reached the Susquehanna River at Peach Bottom, an old river rafting town which had originally been named Ketch Bottom, because of the shallow water at the ferry crossing.

"Peachy" carried produce, passengers, parcels and picnic parties in the years just after the Civil War, following an informal schedule which had no traffic problems. There was only one train.

At one time, optimistic owners thought the Peach Bottom Railroad might extend all the way from Wilmington, Delaware, to York, but their hopes did not mature, the little terminal at Peach Bottom was lost in the rising water when the Conowingo Dam was built, and the little freight cars became scattered through the countryside for use as small farm sheds.

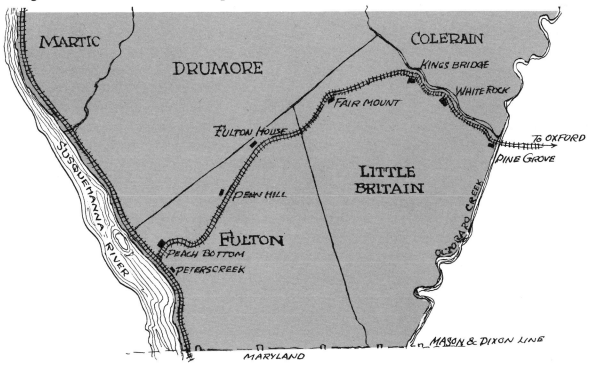

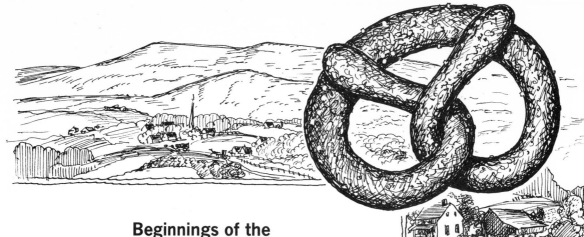

Beginnings of the
Famous Pretzel Industry

As early as 1810, the crisp, brown, salted, twisted pretzel, or "bretzel," became a distinctive bakery product of the Lititz community, and for more than a century remained almost universally with Lititz. Like many early industries, the pretzel bakeries often remained in the same family for generations, and the art of twisting the dough into the familiar shape, which is often associated with folded arms crossed in prayer, became a skill developed by all members of the baker's family.

One of the oldest pretzel bakeries in the country was at Rothsville, near Lititz, and the first pretzel advertising was probably initiated by a travelling pretzel salesman who became known throughout the area as "Dutch Charlie," and who became a familiar figure day after day at homes and taverns, carrying a big basket of freshly baked crisp, warm pretzels.

N. D. Sturgis Pretzel House in Lititz

"Old sports" at Sporting Hill

Sporting Hill, near Manheim, was first called Casseltown, but its name changed after the settlement grew. One of the oldest whiskey distilleries in the county was established there by the Kauffmans, and a tavern was set up near the distillery. It became a favorite haunt for a number of local gentlemen who had acquired the reputation, by their clothes and their behavior, of being "sports," and it is generally believed that the name "Sporting Hill" became associated with the community because of their antics.

Bathtubs were a Real Luxury

In 1839, the report of the Lancaster City Water Works showed that there were nine bathtubs in the city, supplied with water from the Conestoga Creek and the new reservoir at $3.00 per year.

Although bathtubs were scarce, soap was plentiful, because many families made their own soap as one of the regular household chores. A leach barrel or tub had a permanent place somewhere in the yard, to hold wood ashes from the fireplace or stove. Water, or combinations of water with various favorite household dyes or chemicals were poured over the ashes, and, after standing for several weeks, the necessary lye was produced for boiling soap in the big iron kettles that were a familiar household accessory everywhere.

Make Your Own Soap

East Petersburg—East of What?

East Petersburg, between Lancaster and Manheim, had its beginning when Daniel Wolfe, who kept a tavern in the locality, bought a tract of land to lay out a town, and held a lottery to distribute the first lots. The community was established, but nobody bothered to give it a name until some years later when another landowner, Peter Gottshall, added some land to the town and the name Petersburg came into use. However, when mail service through the nation became more efficient, it was discovered that another Petersburg existed in central Pennsylvania. The simplest way to solve the duplication was to call the Lancaster County community East Petersburg, and so it remained to the present time.

Horse Power for the Horse Cars

Passengers travelled by horse-car on the first railroad between Lancaster and Columbia in 1834, but a few weeks later, when the railroad was officially opened between Columbia and Philadelphia, on April 16th, a steam locomotive drew three passenger cars over the entire route, with Governor Wolf and other distinguished guests. The trip from Columbia to Lancaster took one hour.

Street cars in Lancaster were all horsedrawn until 1890. Transportation within the city was supplied by carriage and horse-drawn "omnibus" until 1875, when the first horse cars provided the precedent for the later electric trolleys. The original horse car route led from the railroad station on North Queen Street through a circuit of one or two blocks around the square, and then out the Columbia Pike, and over to the Millersville Pike and Millersville. The conductor frequently had to warn the passengers not to get off when the horses were trotting.

In these days of horse-drawn transportation, hitching-posts and watering troughs for horses were almost as familiar on the streets as modern parking meters, and many homes had a necessary carriage house in the rear instead of a garage, and a mounting block of stone on the front curb.

Davy Crockett Gets into Politics

Davy Crockett, the swash-buckling frontier politician, humorist and teller of tall tales, was only one of many candidates for political office who stopped in Lancaster on various occasions to address their fellow-citizens in the hope of securing their votes. Col. Crockett, of Tennessee, had abandoned his original support of Jackson, and strongly opposed his bank policies, and made his opinion quite evident on a visit to Columbia and Lancaster in the 1830's.

Andrew Jackson had been in Lancaster himself some years before, travelling from York by sleigh in a snowstorm in 1819.

William Henry Harrison, who became President in 1841, visited Lancaster in 1836, and was escorted to the Susquehanna River bridge by Lancaster supporters. President Zachary Taylor, on a tour of the country in 1849, arrived in Lancaster by train, and then continued to Philadelphia. John Marshall, noted Federalist and later Chief Justice of the Supreme Court, was entertained in Lancaster in 1798, after returning from the "XYZ" negotiations in France, and lodged at the *White Swan* Hotel. Daniel Webster, Whig candidate for the Presidency in 1835, visited for several days in Lancaster and Lancaster County.

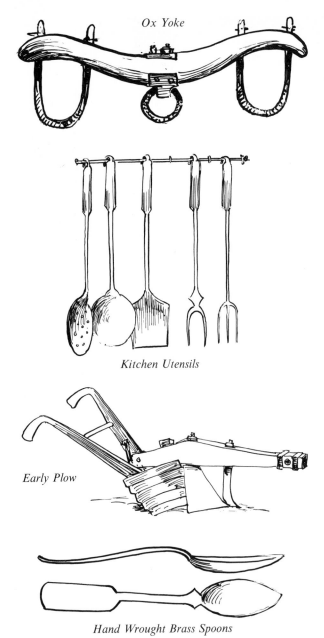

Ox Yoke

Kitchen Utensils

Early Plow

Hand Wrought Brass Spoons

Relics of the Past at Landis Valley

By the middle of the nineteenth century, hand-made tools, agricultural implements and household furnishings were being replaced by factory-made machinery and utensils. Many of the items which had been commonplace for several centuries, such as the spinning wheels, lard-presses, butter-churns, wood-framed plows and cultivators, looms and even home-made mousetraps, were put aside in barns or attics to make room for products of the new industrial age.

Toward the end of the century, two brothers, Henry and George Landis, began to collect and preserve every possible item they could find which represented the rural life of this Pennsylvania area, and stored a vast collection of tools, vehicles, handcraft work, firearms, furniture and utensils, in their barn and house at Landis Valley, a few miles north of Lancaster. The tremendous amount of material, and the many phases of early Pennsylvania farm life which it represented, led to establishment of the Pennsylvania Farm Museum, operated by the Commonwealth of Pennsylvania.

Cow Bells

It is probable that nowhere in the country is there a better actual representation of the life of early America. The blacksmith shop, the gunshop, the collections of heating and cooking equipment, the infinite variety of farm implements, the vehicles of wagon and carriage days, provide a rare opportunity for the visitor to appreciate the ingenuity and craftsmanship of the men and women of old Lancaster and old Pennsylvania.

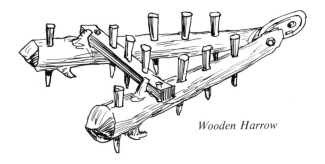

Wooden Harrow

The First Commercial Telegraph

After Professor Morse's experiments with communication by electric telegraph had proved successful in Washington, the first contract for a commercial telegraph line provided for service between Lancaster and Harrisburg, to be completed by January 1, 1846.

With the aid of a Lancaster contractor, wires were strung on crude chestnut poles about a hundred yards apart, with wrappings of gummed cloth on the cross-arms for insulation. On January 1, 1846, the first telegraph instruments arrived in Lancaster, to be operated by a friend of Professor Morse. The relays were wound with very heavy wire, and weighed almost two hundred and fifty pounds each. However, first attempts were unsuccessful, until on January 8, an accidental adjustment to the instruments resulted in a clatter of dots and dashes which represented the first message sent by wire over a commercial telegraph line. It read, "Why don't you write, you rascals?"

There was great interest and excitement about the first telegraph, but not much profit. The Washington office received one cent on their first day of operation, Harrisburg received ten cents, and Lancaster received six and a quarter cents on opening days, all from curiosity to see how a name would appear in dots and dashes. Frequent troubles with the primitive line developed and the instruments would remain in adjustment for only a few minutes at a time. After two months, this first line went out of business, sold the copper wire to pay the operator's expenses, and waited for more public support of telegraphic communication.

The telegraph seemed very mysterious in these first months. Visitors to the office at the North American Hotel were told by a mischievous hotel proprietor that some objects like handkerchiefs, newspapers or stockings could be sent along the wires, and along the roads, travellers kept as far away as possible from the humming wires, for fear the "electricity" might do them some serious harm.

"Old Thad" Stevens

"Old Thad" Stevens, most influential leader of the Republican Party during the Civil War, had moved to Lancaster in 1843, practising law at his office on South Queen Street, and already well known for his reputation as champion of the free public school system in Pennsylvania, and for his opposition to slavery. He was largely responsible for pressure on Lincoln to make the emancipation of slavery a major object of the Civil War, and insisted on a post-war reconstruction policy which would prevent the South from regaining its former power in Congress. His will provided that he should be buried in a cemetery which had no racial discrimination, and his tomb is in Shriner's Cemetery in Lancaster, at West Chestnut and Mulberry Streets.

In 1849, when the Mexican War hero, "Old Rough-and-Ready" Zachary Taylor had been elected to the Presidency, he passed through Lancaster on the way to his inauguration. Thaddeus Stevens of Lancaster had been nominated and elected to Congress on the Whig ticket in the same campaign, and the visit was made the occasion for a grand banquet in the *Swan Hotel* on the Square, where Stevens addressed the gathering of jubilant Whigs.

A few years later, Lancaster Democrats were able to celebrate the nomination and election of their own fellow-citizen, James Buchanan, a political rival of Stevens, to the Presidency.

Citizens Oppose the Fugitive Slave Law at Christiana

The first serious opposition to the new Fugitive Slave Act took place at Christiana in 1851, when runaway slaves were joined by local white citizens in defying a United States Marshal and southern slaveowners who were attempting to recover the slaves. In a bitter fight at the old Parker farmhouse, the slaveowner was killed, his body was hacked and mutilated, and his son and several others were wounded.

Thirty-eight persons were charged with treason, but were found not guilty by a Philadelphia court. Thaddeus Stevens acted as attorney for the defense.

Volunteer Soldiers Prepare to Go to War

The Lancaster Fencibles were one of many county units of volunteer military companies which had organized several years before the Civil War, and answered the call of President Lincoln for 75,000 volunteers in April, 1861.

In both the North and South in the years after the Mexican War, volunteer companies were organized, mostly as social groups, drilling, designing handsome uniforms, parading, holding shooting contests and representing their community in official and gala occasions. At the outbreak of the Civil War, they were among the first to volunteer for three-months service, and the city of Washington was crowded with thousands of gaily uniformed soldiers in the first war months.

The Fencibles—a name which meant home defense—were organized in 1855, and used the upper floor of Fulton Hall as their armory and drill hall. With their own Fencibles' Band, they entertained visiting dignitaries, escorted President-elect Buchanan to Washington and marched in his inaugural parade, and were always a prominent part of community life.

During their three-months service, they were assigned to guard duty at strategic railway points in Maryland, and served under General Patterson near Harper's Ferry during the Manassas campaign, and were mustered out shortly afterwards. These early volunteer companies were then merged with regular regiments, and many of the individual members served with other Pennsylvania Regiments during the war.

Other volunteer units from the county adopted names like the Columbia Rifles, the Marietta Cameron Guard, the Strasburg Cavalry, the Mount Joy Infantry, or the Millersville Home Guard, but the identity of the individual groups was soon lost as the war progressed.

Abraham Lincoln
Speaks in Lancaster

On his way to Washington for his inauguration, Abraham Lincoln came to Lancaster on February 22nd, 1861, leaving his train at the old railroad station at N. Queen and Chestnut Streets, and going across the street to the Caldwell House, later the Hotel Brunswick, for a brief speech to the citizens of Lancaster. About four years later, on April 21, 1865, the funeral train bearing the body of the assassinated President passed through the same location, mourned by the people who had seen and heard him at the start of his administration.

Militia Burn the Columbia Bridge

When the Confederate Army invaded Pennsylvania in 1863, they met with no opposition until they reached the Susquehanna River. Civilian volunteers and militia built and manned rifle pits in Wrightsville to delay the approaching army, and managed to set fire to the long wooden covered bridge just as the Confederates reached the river. The complete destruction of this bridge on June 28th, 1863 stopped Lee's advance toward Philadelphia, and was a significant factor in leading to the great battle at Gettysburg two days later.

Only a few minutes made the difference between the success or failure of Lee's invasion at this point. General Gordon's Confederate troops were the advance of Early's forces, which had occupied York on the previous evening, and if they had succeeded in crossing the bridge into Lancaster County, they would have controlled the railroad lines running to the western armies, and thrown Philadelphia and eastern cities into a state of panic.

The militia had been instructed to delay the enemy long enough to allow a span of the bridge to be blown up by explosives, but the attempt was unsuccessful, and when artillery shells fell into the town, the militia fell back rapidly across the bridge, which burned into complete ruin behind them. Thousands of anxious spectators on the Lancaster banks of the river watched with growing relief on that hot Sunday evening in June, as they saw the Confederate army stranded on the far side of the river, and knew that the invasion would not take place that day. As it happened, the destruction of this bridge made Wrightsville the farthest eastern point of the invasion campaign, for the Confederate troops had to be recalled the next morning, to face the advancing Army of the Potomac, coming north through Maryland.

The Funeral Train of a Martyred President

On April 21st, 1865, a special train with the funeral car heavily draped in black and carrying the body of the martyred President Lincoln passed through Lancaster at the beginning of its sad journey.

The great catafalque in the rotunda of the Capitol at Washington had been visited by many thousands of mourners, all through the day and night of April 20th. On Friday, the 21st, the funeral train moved out of Washington to begin a journey of almost two thousand miles, covering much of the same route which the President-elect had travelled on his way to the White House four years before. In Baltimore, York, Harrisburg and Lancaster, on the first day of the sad journey, buildings were draped in mourning, thousands of citizens gathered at the station or along the tracks, bowed and silent, carrying flowers.

After a stop in Lancaster, the train moved to Philadelphia, where almost a half million mourners viewed the coffin in Independence Hall. Then, through New Jersey, New York, Ohio, and Indiana, the train passed on its way to Springfield, Illinois, where, on May 4th, the coffin was borne to its final resting place.

The first great tragedies in national history —the Civil War and the assassination of a President, rudely awakened a young and adolescent America to a serious realization of the mature responsibilities which now faced a nation which was coming of age.

End of an Era:

Building the Civil War Monument in the Square 1874

A NOTE ABOUT SOURCES

For the reader wishing further detailed information on Lancaster history, the most valuable collection of material is contained in the many publications of the Lancaster County Historical Society, which has printed the results of careful research and the text of many original documents since 1896. The publications are carefully indexed and contain the work of some of Pennsylvania's outstanding historians, of both past and present years.

The only published histories of Lancaster County which contain comprehensive treatment are extremely useful, but unfortunately are no longer in print, although available in libraries. The most recent work, *Lancaster County, Pennsylvania,* edited by H. M. J. Klein, (Lewis Publishing Co., N.Y. 1924. 4 vols.) is an invaluable reference for detailed information. The *History of Lancaster County* by Franklin Ellis and Samuel Evans, (Everts and Peck, Philadelphia, 1883) is the most complete compilation of county history, but it has also been out of print for many years.

Shorter general histories are *Old Lancaster: Tales and Traditions,* by W. F. Worner, (Lancaster, Pa., 1927); *The Story of Lancaster, Old and New,* by William Riddle, (Lancaster, Pa., 1917); and I. D. Rupp, *History of Lancaster County,* (G. Hills, Lancaster, Pa., 1844). The latter is not entirely reliable.

A recent publication, *Historic Heart of Lancaster,* by Gerald S. Lestz, (John Baer's Sons, Lancaster, Pa., 1962) contains an excellent pictorial record of the locations of historic buildings in Lancaster City, and a useful summary of historic events associated with the city. *Lancaster County Since 1841,* by Frederic S. Klein, (Lancaster, Pa., 1955) contains a description of economic and social developments in the city and county, but is no longer in print.

Files of the Lancaster newspapers are essential sources of information, and contain many historical feature articles of significant importance. Special anniversary editions of Lancaster newspapers in 1895, 1927, 1929, 1937 and 1942 have recorded many events from earlier newspaper files. The newspaper files are on microfilm and are available for use for study or research.

Publications by *Community Historians* are available in Lancaster libraries, beginning with the first publications in 1962. They deal particularly with the preservation of local history in the many smaller communities of the county.

Collections of pamphlets, anniversary publications of organizations and institutions, and works related to special areas of local interest are available in the Lancaster County Historical Society, the Fackenthal Library of Franklin and Marshall College, or the Lancaster Free Public Library.

INDEX

OLD LANCASTER: Historic Pennsylvania Community
was designed by William D. Andes *of Lancaster
Pennsylvania. It was lithographed by* Wagaman
Brothers—Printers *of Lititz, Pennsylvania.
The type is Times Roman with News Gothic headings
composed on the Intertype Fotosetter by*
Graphic Services, Inc. *of York, Pennsylvania.*

OLD LANCASTER COUNTY
from an early map of Pennsylvania,
dedicated to Thomas and Richard Penn, proprietors.
By Nicholas Scull, Philadelphia, 1759